The
EVERYTHING®
Divining the Future Book

W9-DDZ-681

Dear Reader:

If you've just picked up this book, you're wondering now if you can really divine the future. Let me assure you—it's for real. And you don't need to study with the masters in ancient China to learn the I Ching, nor rub shoulders with the nobility of nineteenth-century Italy in order to grab hold of the Tarot—it's all right here in this book.

Having grown up as the infinite idealist, I never shunned the idea of "happily ever after." And divination, you should know, makes this concept just a little more achievable. From fairy tales to real-life magic, from love and romance to career success, divination is a tool that has been used since the beginning of mankind because, quite simply, it works.

The truth is, one of the richer aspects of life is in the possibilities it offers you. Once you know what lies before you, you can begin attaining your goals. And divination is always about bringing your dreams to fruition . . . making the dark unconscious conscious. This book and divination won't fall short of your expectations. Go to it!

Warm regards,

Jenni Kosarin

The EVERYTHING® Series

Editorial

Publishing Director	Gary M. Krebs
Managing Editor	Kate McBride
Copy Chief	Laura MacLaughlin
Acquisitions Editor	Bethany Brown
Development Editor	Julie Gutin
Production Editor	Khrysti Nazzaro

Production

Production Director	Susan Beale
Production Manager	Michelle Roy Kelly
Series Designers	Daria Perreault
	Colleen Cunningham
Cover Design	Paul Beatrice
	Frank Rivera
Layout and Graphics	Colleen Cunningham
	Rachael Eiben
	Michelle Roy Kelly
	Daria Perreault
	Erin Ring
Cover Artist	Rosanne Raneri
Interior Illustrations	Barry Littmann

Visit the entire Everything® Series at everything.com

THE

EVERYTHING®

DIVINING THE FUTURE BOOK

From runes to Tarot cards
and tealeaves to crystals—
predict what fate has in store for you

Jenni Kosarin

Adams Media Corporation
Avon, Massachusetts

An Everything® Series Book.
Everything® is a registered trademark of Adams Media Corporation.

Published by Adams Media Corporation
57 Littlefield Street, Avon, MA 02322 U.S.A.
www.adamsmedia.com

ISBN: 1-58062-866-4
Printed in the United States of America.

J   I   H G F E D C B A

Library of Congress Cataloging-in-Publication Data
Kosarin, Jenni.
The everything divining the future book / Jenni Kosarin.
    p.   cm.   (Everything series)
        ISBN 1-58062-866-4
1. Divination. I. Title: Divining the future book. II. Title.
            II. Series.
        BF1773.K67   2003
        133.3–dc21   2003000374

This book is available at quantity discounts for bulk purchases.
For information, call 1-800-872-5627.

Contents

Acknowledgments

Love to Donna and Paul Kosarin, who give the words "resourceful" and "supportive" higher meaning. A grateful tip of the hat as well to Randy Jones, the most incredible Tarot reader this side of the universe; to Alessandro Brandoni for his clever palm readings; to Malin Hammar, a special woman and healer whom I'm privileged to call friend; and to Gisela Stramer, owner of the spiritual well-being spa of Grand Hotel Palazzo Della Fonte in Fiuggi, Italy, for her beautiful meditation techniques.

A very special thanks also to acquisitions editor Bethany Brown, who shaped and created the vision of the book and devotedly encouraged it through the entire process, and Julie Gutin, development editor at Adams, who has the talent as well as the required amount of patience to indulge an author's madcap affinities and make it all look good. Thank you all!

Top Ten Divination Methods
You Will Learn in This Book

1. **Tarot cards:** From the Death card to The Fool, find out how these cards fit together and what they really mean for your destiny.

2. **I Ching:** Learn a fascinating ancient Chinese divination method as it was written in the Book of Changes.

3. **Runes:** This old Nordic alphabet is spiritual and mystical and can be used for divination as well as meditation.

4. **Astrology:** Find out the mysteries of your future and your potential according to your sun sign.

5. **Numerology:** Predict which days you should stay out of fate's way and which days you'll soar!

6. **Feng shui:** A little simple rearranging goes a long way for changing your luck in finance, health, and love.

7. **Tealeaf reading:** You don't have to be a gypsy to learn how to divine through tealeaves or coffee grounds.

8. **Crystals:** For looking into the future or for boosting your good energy, no good psychic goes without her crystals.

9. **Dream interpretation:** Finally understand what your strange and curious nighttime fantasies are all about.

10. **Palmistry:** By analyzing patterns, shapes, and marks on your hands, you can see where your future is really leading you.

Introduction

▶YOU ENTER AN OLD PSYCHIC SHOP and see a mysterious "gypsy" woman with jangling bracelets, hoop earrings, and a multicolor turban. Lights from the candles flicker around her, casting curious shadows. You think you see a black cat sitting beside her. You smell jasmine incense and something musty.

Suddenly, the woman speaks. "Come closer!" You move closer, albeit with a bit of uncertainty. "Tell me. Tell me what you want to know," she whispers huskily. "Madame Bovart will now tell you everything you want to know." And with a pass of a hand over her crystal ball, she begins. Can she really see into your future?

Since the beginning of time, people have always been fascinated by the idea of seeing into the future. Though it may seem far-fetched, we do it all the time. Wall Street brokers do it every day as they try to predict the movement of the market. All of us in our daily lives analyze patterns and trends that help us make predictions as to what the future holds. And that's what fortunetelling is all about. Through analyzing patterns and trends, ancient signs and symbols, we're able to get a glimpse of the future. There is one big difference, though. Divination has been around a lot longer than Wall Street.

In fact, divination has existed since before recorded time. It can be traced back more than 30,000 years. Shamanism, for example, is one of the oldest practices of divination. It originated in Siberia and the Far East, and spread to North America, where it is still practiced by Native Americans. The art involves talking to spirits and interpreting the sounds and movements of animals.

Another ancient method of divination, numerology, was developed in the Mediterranean region and was shaped by Pythagoras, a Greek philosopher and mathematician (sixth century B.C.). Ancient Chinese divination, on the other hand, was derived from tradition, philosophy, and science, through the wisdom of oracular judgments of the I Ching (The Book of Changes) some 3,000 years ago. And many believe that Tarot was influenced by the mystical Hebrew teachings of the Kabbalah. (For instance, Kabbalah is based on the twenty-two paths and the Tarot consists of twenty-two Major Arcana.) Ancient Persian divination tools ranged from the use of omens to palmistry. And the Northern Europeans developed an alphabet of runes, which the Nordic people used for writing and divination as far back as 100 B.C.

Divination evolved throughout the ages with the help of magicians and psychics, but philosophers and scientists were also very much involved. For example, ancient Greek philosophers Plato and Socrates were adherents of Pythagorean principles. And the work of Sigmund Freud made leaps and bounds in helping us look into the subconscious mind as well as the hidden intricacies of sleep and dreaming. Carl Gustav Jung, at one time associated with Freud, wrote and analyzed the role of "meaningful coincidence" and how it was to be applied to our lives. He believed that life events do not happen by chance, but by the merging of time, matter, space, thought, and spirit. Essentially, this means that coincidences, according to Jung, really do have higher meaning.

Divination allows you to see all of the possibilities of life, and forces you to live life to the fullest. There is an old Sanskrit proverb from a famous Buddhist swami named Vivekananda, who said: "It is the coward and the fool who says 'This is fate.' But it is the strong man who stands up and says 'I will make my fate.'" Facing your fate is what the art of divination is really about. And who wouldn't love to know what's going to happen in the next few weeks, months, or years?

The real trick is to use this gift of information in a positive way. This book offers you this gift in the form of a quick guide to methods of divination, with all of its wisdom and helpful hints, charted and written down through the ages. After reading *The Everything® Divining the Future Book*, you will be able to master the art of divining the future and unlock the key to the mysteries of the universe. Remember, you do have the power within you to make your fate and put yourself on the right path to happiness! Ⓔ

Chapter 1

The Basics of Divination

Maybe you'd like to learn fortune-telling to help you make important life decisions. Or maybe you think it would be fun to be able to tell the future for your friends. Divination can give you both—serious answers as well as lots of enjoyment. Just remember: The psychics and fortunetellers you may look to for wisdom and advice were once like you—they, too, needed to learn and perfect their craft before putting a sign up on the door. All the information you'll need to begin is included in this chapter.

Fate and Predetermined Destiny

Is our destiny predetermined? Yes and no. You do have a life lesson that you need to learn in this lifetime. However, the path you choose to get to that knowledge is up to you—and the possibilities along the way are infinite.

Choice and free will always exist in life, and you should never look to divination for set facts. What divination *can* do is show you the possibilities and offer you the guidance you might need for the future. Think of divination as a friend or a mentor. In the end, the way you choose to live your life is up to you.

The concept of "fate" comes from Western philosophy, and is derived from three religions: Christianity, Judaism, and Islam. In different ways, each teaches that a person's life is influenced by governing forces over which they have no control.

What do you choose to make your reality? If you have your cards read and the Tarot card reader tells you that you'll meet your love in four months' time, are you going to sit home every night, watching television and waiting for the phone to ring? Of course not. Sure, it's possible that you could meet that person after a year, by chance, in an elevator or on the subway, but why wait? Good things won't happen unless you're ready for them. For example, if someone tells you that you will be famous one day and you take no steps to advance your career, what can you expect? Get ready, get set, and get out there!

Also, remember to take everything with a grain of salt. If you're worried about your health, don't go to a psychic in order to find out what's wrong. One woman had a small lump in her breast and asked a psychic about it. The psychic told her not to worry, that it was nothing, benign; so she never went to the doctor to have it checked. Later it was confirmed to be cancerous. Always get a second opinion and never go to a psychic for medical advice. That's what doctors are for!

Too many people make the mistake of taking what a psychic tells them as "truth" and changing their lives to the point of destruction. Beware of bringing incredibly important matters to a psychic and trusting what that one person tells you.

Finding Your Path

Eventually, you will learn your lesson and you will experience what you need to, and your experience will enhance and strengthen your soul and your purpose—your reason for being here. Everyone has a life purpose. What would happen if we were all Einsteins or Mozarts? We'd have a whole lot of people doing physics and writing music, but no one to actually implement the scientific theories or perform the musical pieces.

Everyone has a role in the world and contributes to the workings of the universe, so that it continues to exist in harmony. Granted, our world doesn't always seem very harmonious—there is still a lot of pain and suffering caused by wars, conflicts, diseases, and natural disasters. That is why it is so important to know what your role is in the world, so that you can make it a better place in which to live. The key is to figure out where you want to go and how you're going to get there. Once you know, divination can be a great tool to help nudge you forward in the right direction.

How Destiny Works

To give you a very basic example of destiny and predisposition, let's take your teeth. That's right—your teeth. You can brush your teeth five times a day and floss like a maniac, but you may still get cavities. Why? It may be that you are genetically predisposed to cavities. On the other hand, there are a few people who don't take care of their teeth and yet hardly ever have any problems—not even a single cavity in their entire lifetime. Why do these people have fewer cavities when the rest of us have a mouth full of them, though we brush and floss regularly? Science can give you a more detailed explanation as to which hereditary traits might contribute to having healthy teeth, but the point of the matter is, some people have them and some people don't—it's something you were born with. Can we say that you are predestined to have healthy or unhealthy teeth? In a way, yes, we can.

And if it is true that some of us were born with good teeth while others were born with a photographic memory, and still others have great musical ability—and, in fact, so far scientists have not found a genetic explanation for these types of traits—isn't it possible that each and every one of us is born with a specific destiny in mind?

Is Divination for Real?

Of course, scientists will argue until they're blue in the face that if something can't be proven, it's simply not valid. This may be true. But even today, in the twenty-first century (and with all our scientific research), not all the questions have been answered. No one can tell us when an earthquake will happen. They can only tell us (again, from patterns and study) where it is likely to eventually happen. Divination, in the same way, relies on belief, faith, and research. It resembles science because it is also a method derived from recognized patterns and studies done throughout history.

But how do we know it's real? We just do. There are many cynics who doubt the possibility of peering into the future and seeing what's going to happen. But a good psychic does not claim to be able to see the future as if it is set in stone. What he can do is look at the momentous, life-changing events such as a major career change or a second marriage you were destined for—events that will happen in your life if they're meant to happen.

FACT

Albert Einstein, one of the greatest minds of our time, said with quick wit, "Reality is merely an illusion, albeit a very persistent one." He also stated, "Great spirits have always found violent opposition from mediocre minds. The latter cannot understand it when a man does not thoughtlessly submit to hereditary prejudices but honestly and courageously uses his intelligence."

If you want proof, look around you. Some of us were born into this lifetime with extraordinary luck with certain things. Others will suffer constantly in love; still others will become famous; and a number of us will live, contentedly or not, our normal, routine life, going to work and coming home to our families every day. But everyone—rich or poor, outgoing or shy, happy or not so happy—will learn the things they need to learn to fulfill their destiny.

How Divination Works

People who are skeptics of how divination is done always ask the same questions. For instance: "If I have my Tarot cards read every day, it will say something different. How can all of it be true?" Well, you should never have your Tarot cards read every day—once a month or every couple of months is sufficient.

How often you should rely on divination depends on the method you use. For instance, you can use numerology and crystals (when used for meditation or healing) every day. I Ching can help you solve everyday problems as well as those that are life-affecting. Runes can steer you in the right direction for small questions or for meditation, but should not be consulted every day. You also should not use a crystal ball daily, because it is meant only for scrying (tapping into the future). Palmistry provides a general guide to your character, your personality, and your life destiny, but because the lines of your hands will not quickly change their shapes, you should not use this method very often.

Back to the Question

The reason the Tarot cards can change what they say every day is because everything you do in your life changes your possibilities for the future. For instance, you go to a psychic Tarot card reader and she tells you that your career is going well and you will have the opportunity for advancement in about three months. The next day you have a tiff with your supervisor or you say something to rub a colleague the wrong way. This little scene can alter your near future.

Does that mean that you should steer clear of everyone and watch every small move you make? Sit behind your desk and worry? Of course not. This is simply how fate operates. Sometimes it's not even up to you. It could be something as simple as the director of human resources receiving a letter from the head of the company, unbeknownst to you, saying that there is no money in the budget right now to promote even the more deserving of candidates.

All destinies interconnect and pass through one another before they play out as actual events, so you need to find the time when your destiny is least affected by short-term factors (timing is covered in greater detail in Chapter 4). All of this explains why Tarot cards may tell you something different from one day to the next.

Changing Destiny and Karma

The key to living with your destiny is to avoid excessive worrying and not try to control it. Controlling and manipulating your destiny is the surest way to land flat on your face. You'll still have to learn your lessons. And it might just be more difficult for you. Be kind to yourself. Search for help when you need it. And don't try to stifle your suffering—feel it and live it so you can continue on, learn, and live a happier life. If you constantly avoid it, it will eventually find you anyway. This is what we sometimes call "karma."

In Buddhism, karma is the idea that "what goes around comes around"—that your fate and your future are determined by your past. If you lived your past life by the rules of the universe and were kind and helpful to others, you are rewarded in your next life. If you did not, your next life is more difficult.

Karma Chrome

The Buddhist view of karma assumes that our present positions in life are the result of justice and retribution. Some Western philosophers say that the Eastern view of karma helps those in power, who can pat themselves on the back for having good karma. In Western teachings, karma is more about cause and effect within a particular lifetime and does not require belief in reincarnation. It is the energy around you, at this moment or period in time. If you spread the good energy through good deeds, it will come back to you—it's like catching a good wave if you're surfing. It works for the little things in life, like having the instinct to pick a winning number, meeting and connecting with a person who might help you in the future, performing a presentation well on a certain day, and so on. Of course, karma is not foolproof—anyone can have a bad day. Sometimes, it has more to do with your destiny than with the details of everyday life.

FACT

Buddhism is not the only tradition that includes belief in reincarnation. Other ancient cultures that adhered to this belief were the Hindu, Gaulish, Celtic, Druid, Greek (Pythagorean), Mayan, Incan, and Egyptian.

The best thing you can do to make your destiny work for you is to be good to yourself and to the people around you, and to pace yourself—indulge sometimes and cut back other times. Search for friendships, work, and play that bring out the best in you. Your karmic lessons will find you in this lifetime and teach you the things you need to know.

So You Want to Learn Fortunetelling

Perhaps you've passed by the Tarot card reader's window down the street and you're wondering if she's for real or a phony. Should you trust her with your future? Or maybe you've been in the New Age section of your local bookstore a million times. You've wanted to learn the mysteries behind this art called divination, but you never knew where to start. Well, you're on the right track. Just holding this book in your hands will get you there—every nuance, skill, and technique for foretelling the future is here. Read the material, study the methods, and try it out on anyone who lets you. If you really want to learn, it won't take you long before you'll be able to do it yourself.

What You'll Need

To master divination, all you need are knowledge, patience, instinct, and practice. Read through all of the chapters, take notes, and then decide which divination system you want to try first. Make sure to focus on that system and get lots of practice. As you'll soon find out, friends, family, and colleagues will be asking you incessantly to divine their future. Take advantage. The more you do it, the better your skills will become.

ALERT!

Some people were born with excessively good instinct while the rest of us have to work at it, but it's inherent in human nature and we all have it. Whether you're looking at the symbols in tealeaves, the Tarot, or even runes, let your mind wander and your subconscious take over. You may be surprised by what comes out.

Sometimes the easiest way to grasp a concept quickly is by watching it being done. Think of all the cooking shows on television today! It would be simple enough to pick up a cookbook and put theory into action (the book is always needed anyway as a good reference point), but there's something about watching someone else do it before your eyes. So do yourself a favor and go to someone who knows what he's doing. Even if you get the sense that your mentor is not telling you anything important or useful, you'll be shocked at how much you take away from the experience.

The Internet is also a helpful tool for learning more about fortunetelling and divination. However, be wary of charlatans who may give you bad advice. Remember—anyone can post truths, half-truths, and plain lies on the Net, so take everything with a grain of salt.

Developing Psychic Powers

Being psychic does not mean you can predict the winning lottery numbers before they're drawn. If that were true, psychics certainly wouldn't be sitting around waiting to tell you your future. People always ask why psychics can't predict world tragedies, wars, or the death of a major icon or political figure before they happen. They also ask why bad luck sometimes happens to good psychics. Why don't they see it beforehand and do something to prevent it?

There are many ways to explain these questions, but let's first define the expression. "Being psychic" simply means that you are at harmony with the energy around you—tuned in to signs, symbols, and coincidences of the universe. Have you ever found yourself talking on the telephone while the television was on, when all of sudden a program caught your attention? Your subconscious was listening, even though you weren't.

"Being psychic" works in a similar fashion. Psychics are simply aware of the inner voices that speak to them; they listen to their hunches and are attuned to shifts in the surrounding energy. It's all too common for psychics to be able to read the future for other people, but not for themselves—when it comes to their own life, they have no idea what may happen the following day.

The reason for this is that in order to be psychic, you must remove the subjective and be completely objective—without judgment, prejudice, or rationalization. To silence the ego, we rely on the aids such as the Tarot cards or runes, which help us to navigate through the energy that flows into and out of them. We then translate this energy and make our predictions.

Good Psychics Gone Wrong

Good psychics sometimes make bad predictions. The reason for this is the human ability to exercise free will. Each person has the power to change his fate, and to affect the world and its history. We are all part of a bigger picture—what each of us does every day affects the outcome of future events on a global scale. A psychic can only see what will happen if we continue along the path we're on right now. If we all do something significant to change that path, the fate of the world will change as well.

FACT

Nostradamus (Michel de Nostredame) was a French physician and astrologer who lived from 1503 to 1566. Back in his day, Nostradamus hid his predictions by disguising them in code, perhaps to protect himself from possible attacks of the Church. His book of prophecies, written hundreds of years ago, is still selling well today.

Tapping into Your Psychic Ability

When you are psychic, you are also said to be "clairvoyant," or clear-seeing. You can see events from the past, present, or future. This requires intense focus and concentration. One of the best ways you can get in touch with your psychic self is to practice techniques of relaxation, meditation, and visualization. The following exercise can help you do just that:

1. Sit up straight in a chair with your feet planted firmly on the ground. Close your eyes if that helps you to focus.
2. Breathe in deeply and exhale three or four times, then continue breathing evenly.
3. Visualize a spiral of light going around you. It starts at your feet, goes up to the top of your head, and then slowly moves back down again.
4. Imagine that this light is from a heavenly force, protecting and shielding you like a cocoon. Trust the spiral of light around you, and feel every part of your body relaxing and warming to it.
5. Now, move the light so that it's spiraling through your body, up and down, fifteen times.
6. Keeping the spiral going, also imagine a different fixed beam of light starting in your chest region, near your heart, going up to the top of your head.
7. Now concentrate and think of one particular person you're going to send this light to. In your mind, make a question to that person.
8. Send out the light and wait for the response, letting it come to you when it's ready.

Open your eyes. Did you get an answer? What were the feelings that came to you immediately? As you start getting in tune with the energy around you, you will be able to connect with anyone in this world or beyond. Remember to always send strong, positive, loving thoughts. Only use your gifts for beautiful and spiritual reasons.

ALERT!

In the beginning, you should practice using a person who knows you are going to get in touch with him—someone you can speak with on the phone later to check your results. Tell a friend you're going to contact him at a particular time. Ask him to remember how he felt at that moment and see if the feeling you perceived, sitting in your chair, was correct.

Extra-Sensory Perception (ESP) and Intuition

Here is another very common question: "What is the difference between ESP and intuition?" Basically, intuition is what you need first, before you can develop extra-sensory perception. ESP is simply that—an extra perception you can practice and learn to summon at will. Humans normally have five stable senses: sight, hearing, touch, smell, and taste. It is often said that when a person is blind or deaf, her other faculties are sharper and more attuned. Those who cannot see must rely on the other four senses; with practice, these senses grow and develop. The same is true of ESP—the more you rely on it and the more you use it, the more attuned you will become.

Have you ever experienced ESP? For example, have you ever had any of the following experiences?

- You got a hunch that something was going to happen, and it did.
- You had a sudden urge to go somewhere and when you arrived, it turned out that someone there needed you.

- You knew for certain how a friend felt even though she tried to hide her feelings from you.
- You were humming a tune and then turned on the radio, and that same song was playing.
- You had a strange reaction to a friend who seemed to be trying to help you; later, you found out that he really did have bad intentions in mind.
- You sometimes get the feeling that there is a presence near you, aiding you, and everything you do at the moment turns out well.
- You had something bad happen to you and experienced a kind of calm, immediately understanding the tragedy's unseen benefit.

If you have ever found yourself in any of these situations, you have probably experienced ESP—most of us have at some point in our lives. Psychics are only different because they learn how to use their knowledge in a more concentrated way. They trust that hunch and their inner voice, believing that there is no such thing as coincidence. You can become an expert as well. The difference between them and you is only experience! Ⓔ

Chapter 2

Divining with Confidence

Congratulations! You're ready to begin. Now the question is, What's out there? There are many different methods of divination, and you can use as few or as many as you feel comfortable with. There are no right or wrong choices. In this chapter, you'll find out which methods work best in certain situations and which types of divination may be right for you, as well as other helpful hints for becoming a confident fortuneteller.

Which Method Is Right for You?

The right method is the one that inspires you. Does the Tarot touch your soul? Does I Ching make you anxious? Does divination by runes bring out your intuition and creativity? The one way to know is to try them all and see what you're good at. As you read this chapter, make a mental note as to which types of divination you think would best suit you and your needs. Then, try them all. You can't lose!

When you're practicing divination, also keep in mind that you're stepping into unknown territory. There's no one there to tell you whether or not you're doing it in the most effective way, so you'll need strength, perseverance, a good sense of humor, and patience. Take your time and don't rush it. The more curious you are, the faster you'll learn. Think of the energy you put in as time well spent. Eventually, you will understand all there is to know about tasseography, astrology, palmistry, and the various other types of divination.

Here are some of the more common tools of fortunetelling:

- **Beginner:** Numerology, astrology, Tarot, lithomancy (crystals)
- **Intermediate:** Tasseography (tealeaf reading), chiromancy (palmistry), runes, oneiromancy (divining dreams)
- **Advanced:** I Ching, psychometry (divining by using objects or possessions), crystallomancy (crystal ball reading)

This list is merely a basic compilation that can give you a better idea of what's in store. It's possible that you'll try out I Ching, listed under "advanced," and discover that it's the most agreeable system for you. Symbols and interpretation can seem daunting at first, but don't get discouraged. When you put your heart into it and develop the right mindset, looking into the future will be a snap.

The Price of Success

One thing you may want to take into consideration when choosing a method of divination is cost. In order to read Tarot cards, for example, you'll need to go out and buy your own set. Throughout this book, references are made to the Rider-Waite Tarot deck, but there are hundreds of different types of Tarot decks out there! Each one is elaborately made, beautiful and mystical, and you may find one that inspires you in particular. Will you be able to afford it? Probably. Some Tarot decks cost only about ten dollars, though others may be much pricier.

The most expensive investment that you could make in divination is a crystal ball—they are quite costly. Another expensive investment is a collection of crystals, for which you may have to pay a large sum. On the other hand, getting a set of runes is much cheaper. In fact, many psychics advise beginners to make their own runes—not because it costs less, but because the act of making them helps absorb your energy, and the runes become more attuned to you. Other affordable forms of fortunetelling include tasseography (all you need is some tea), palmistry, numerology, astrology, dream divination, and psychometry.

What You Need to Know

Any question you have may be adapted to most types of fortunetelling, but some of these methods may be more appropriate for particular kinds of questions. For a general reading, your best bet is Tarot cards or I Ching. To look in the near future, you can use runes, crystals, psychometry, or dream divination. To look farther down the line, into the long-term future, you can choose from numerology, palmistry, or crystallomancy (crystal ball reading). Also consider the question and how it relates to a particular area of your life. To answer relationship questions, for example, you may want to use Tarot or astrology. For questions regarding your career, try the Tarot, I Ching, or numerology.

Narrow It Down

Another way to pick the best divination tool for you is to look for a method that matches your own character traits. Are you emotional? Sensitive? Spontaneous? Or are you more practical? Analytical? Reserved? Some tools of divination require psychological insight in order to find hidden meaning behind the archaic symbols and codes. Other methods call for less intuition. To get an idea of which type of fortunetelling might be best suited for you, take the following personality quiz.

- Have you got a knack for psychology? Do you like giving advice? Are you quick to forgive because you understand the motives behind why people do the things they do? If you answered yes to one of these, you are an Analyzer. Analyzers will do well with oneiromancy (divining dreams), lithomancy (using crystals), or I Ching.
- Are you more rational? Practical? Do you rely more on statistics than on intuition? Are you more comfortable with certainties than with the unknown? If that's the case, you are probably a Fact Finder. Precision and a detail-oriented mind are essential traits for formula-type methods of divination. Numerology, astrology, feng shui, and palmistry would work best for you.
- Do you feel like you're on this planet only half the time? Do you tend to be moody? Romantic? Do people sometimes call you idealistic and constantly advise you to keep two feet on the ground? If this is more your cup of tea, you are a Dreamer. Try tasseography (tealeaf reading), the Tarot, and the runes.
- Do you make decisions in your life based solely on intuition and strong hunches? Do you feel everything deeply, and immediately know the higher purpose of it? Do you emphatically believe in fate? If you know that you are psychic, you are obviously a Born Psychic. Here are the tools meant for you: psychometry (using an object or possession); crystallomancy (using a crystal ball); interpreting life symbols and coincidences; and necromancy (channeling spirits during séances or through the Ouija board).

Additional Options

What do you think so far? If you still haven't found anything interesting, here are some other common forms of divination:

- **Dowsing:** Locating anything from water to lost properties under the earth.
- **Phrenology:** Reading bumps and indentations on the head.

- **Graphology:** Determining the character and future of a person through her handwriting.
- **Clairaudience:** Like clairvoyance (seeing into the future), this is done when you hear sounds or voices ahead of time.
- **Geomancy:** Divining using any substance of the earth—sand or soil, for example.
- **Pyromancy:** Predicting future events through fire.

FACT

There are hundreds of types of divination used today, and some are stranger than others. Here are two interesting examples: Tyromancy is divination by reading the texture and cracks in cheese. Cromniomancy involves looking at the layers of an onion to see into the future.

Know Your Audience

Once you have chosen your divination method, you also need to consider your audience. Everyone and their second cousin twice removed will request a reading. Are you ready?

It's good to practice as much as you can, but remember that you are not required to read for everyone. Let's say your sister is a real skeptic and thinks that divination is nothing but baloney—and yet she, too, wants her cards read. You're not obligated to do it. The right thing to do here might just be to politely decline. Keep in mind that when you do readings for people who cast a haze of doubt around them, only half of the reading comes out the way it should. Sometimes it can even backfire on the pessimist.

Divination tools can be quirky in that they really feed off the surrounding energy. Strangely enough, energy has a sense of humor, too. Worse, you may invoke negative energy if you do a reading while you are in a bad mood or angry. Be careful! Do readings only when the tone of the situation is encouraging. You're giving a part of yourself when you read for someone. Make sure it's a gift they appreciate.

Readings for Yourself

Can you do readings for yourself? Sure you can. The question is—should you? On the upside, who knows you better than you? Chances are, if a card that comes out has five interpretations, you will instantly know what it's referring to. But this can be a downside, too. It's human nature to choose things to our advantage. For instance, if one card can mean both happiness and superficiality, which meaning do you think you'll pick? Be honest. You can't do a good reading for yourself unless you can be totally objective.

It's Tempting

The truth is, anyone who reads cards or casts runes will admit that they've read for themselves at least once, even if they don't do it anymore. One of the reasons why you shouldn't read for yourself is that it may become addictive. When people realize that they are doing readings every single day, they know it's time to stop. It's dangerous to be dependent on readings for every single decision you need to make in the course of everyday life. And it's even more dangerous to keep trying again until you get the result that you secretly desired.

Learning how to tap into the mysteries of the universe brings power. If you can achieve a good balance of that power, you can read for yourself. But if you use this power to control and manipulate your life, you're on the wrong track. Be good to yourself, and set boundaries. Perhaps the best solution here would be to choose one day of the month when you're going to read your cards or throw the I Ching coins. That way, you won't be led astray.

ALERT!

Don't rush! If your friend comes to you with ten minutes to spare and asks you to do a reading, you should probably say no. You need time to set up the reading, get the mood right, and concentrate. Even if he wants to pick "just one card," tell him you'd prefer doing it another time.

What You Need to Explain

You sit down. You're just about to cast runes for a friend. She's got a strange, perturbed, "what did I get myself into?" look on her face. The lights are dim, the candles are lit, and you're ready. What next? You must now explain to her how divination works—in detail.

It's important to remember that this step is mandatory. You need to repeat it each time you do a reading for someone. Why? Two reasons: To protect them and to protect yourself.

Remember what you learned in Chapter 1 about fate and destiny? Well, the person you are divining for needs to learn that, too. The most important thing for all parties to understand when practicing divination is that destiny is what you make of it. Free will always exists. Making sure that this point is understood before the reading begins will take the pressure off you as well as the other person.

Providing the right information and remaining objective is key to any good reading. Let's say you're reading for your friend Joanne. She's looking to you for advice on her boyfriend. Give it—objectively—based on the cards, not what you think. Throughout the reading, you must forget that you think he's the world's biggest jerk. Only read what the cards tell you. And be sure to let her know that you're telling her the future based on the way things are going presently. If she does something drastic tomorrow, her future will change, too.

Protecting Those You Read For

For fun, let's dramatize the situation. Let's say that Joanne has a wonderful boyfriend—a real saint—who loves and adores her. She wants to know if they're going to get married. You're reading her Tarot cards, and the Four of Wands (or the Ten of Cups in some cases—one of the two "marriage" cards), comes out in her future. "Yes!" you exclaim. "He's the one you're going to marry!"

Your friend is thrilled. In fact, she's so happy that the very next day she tells everyone she knows that she's going to marry her boyfriend, Barry. A few hours later, Barry is congratulated by seven friends (and his own mother) on his impending wedding. Wedding? What wedding? *My* wedding? Barry is not amused. In fact, he's livid. He loses his temper, and the couple has a fight. Subsequently, Barry breaks up with Joanne.

This is a classic example of how *not* to react to a reading. Joanne let the reading influence her life too much—and changed the way things were going. What Joanne should have done was take note of the information and keep it to herself. It's your job as the reader to make sure Joanne understands the way destiny works. This way, your friend is protected and she won't do something stupid—like registering for wedding gifts before she's been proposed to.

QUESTION?

How much information should I get before doing a reading?
Get all the information you can. If you comprehend the question better, you'll understand the responses better. A common mistake people make is not giving the psychic any background information because they want to see if the psychic can "guess" their situation. In the end, these people are just wasting everyone's time.

Protecting Yourself

Here's another situation. Your colleague Steven comes to you for advice on his career. He tells you that he senses there's no room for him to grow in his current position. He wants to know if he's in a dead-end job. This is a real stickler for you. Consider the possibilities: If you tell him yes, he may quit, and you'd be responsible; if you tell him no, he would stick around and waste his time in a job that won't go anywhere—and you'd be responsible as well.

What's the solution? You need to explain to him that a person may take many different paths. Tell him that you'll read for him but, in the end, it's his decision. And let him know that the future is not set in stone. This way he's protected, you're protected, and you don't have to carry around a burden of guilt for the rest of your life.

How to Ask Good Questions

If you want a good reading, ask a good question. Steven's question, "Should I leave my current job?" isn't very appropriate. Why? First, it's not a yes/no question, even though it seems to be. A real yes/no question only has two possible answers. This question, though, has several potential responses:

- Yes, but you won't be happy.
- Yes, but your next job won't be better.
- Yes, but your wife will leave you for the plumber.

You get the point. So how do you get a more precise answer? Ask a more precise question. A proper reading offers answers such as "Yes, stay with it but you need to be more aggressive with your work," or "Yes, stay with it for now and search for another job in the meantime." Instead of asking one big question, get your friend to ask many more specific questions. Narrow it down, and you'll get good results.

Be Specific

Make a general question more specific. Here are some examples to use as alternatives to Steven's inquiry:

1. At this moment, does my boss see potential for me in the company? (Note: It's important to include the phrase "at this moment," as the situation may change.)
2. Is there another job more suited for me at this company?
3. Do I have a shot at it?
4. If no, what do I need to do to have a chance? (Divination has the power to help you make a change with good advice that puts fate into your own hands. If you use it, you won't be let down.)
5. Should I talk to my boss about my future with the company?
6. What does my boss think about me as an employee?
7. Can I trust my colleagues? (Ask about each colleague separately.)
8. Is it possible I'll get a raise in the next three months?

The point here is not to ask one of these questions, but to ask all of them. Only then can you determine the answer to Steven's original question.

Predicting with Accuracy

These days, divination is more of a practice than a theory. Because it's been around for thousands of years, symbols and interpretations have been passed down and confirmed anew by many different cultures. But besides relying on the mountain of material out there, you should also trust your own hunches. How do you get to the point where your readings are on the mark? Aside from practice, there are three areas on which you can focus: You need to know what to look for, be able to recognize patterns, and get feedback. Don't worry! When you're getting good at predicting with accuracy, you'll know it.

Know What to Look For

Here's the secret good readers never tell you. When the querent (the term psychics use for the person for whom you are doing a reading) asks the question, the psychic first determines if it's answerable. How do you, the psychic, do that? You decide which cards, runes, or crystals, specifically, would give them a definite, clear response of yes or no. If the question cannot be answered accurately, you help the querent re-form the question.

Know what you're looking for and, when these cards appear, you'll know your reading is accurate. It's better to take the time beforehand rather than to try to make the answer fit the question later.

Before you lay the cards out or make the crystal circle, you should decide what you're looking for and what it will mean. This is the most important part of doing a reading and doing it well. For example, let's say you're doing a Tarot card reading for your friend Rachel. She asks, "Will I have future stability in my current job?" Before you lay the cards out, think. Which cards are you hoping to find in the "future" column when you put the cards down? Which cards signify stability in work matters? Pentacles! The Nine and Ten of Pentacles are the strongest money and stability cards. If they show up in the reading, you know your answer is a definite yes.

Yes/No Questions

Certain questions can be answered with a definite yes or no and have "one card" answers. But if you don't find that one card, you should still interpret the cards that you do get, though the results won't be definite. For example, the Devil card has many interpretations. One of them is karma and destiny. If your friend Rachel asks if she and her boyfriend are not just meant for each other, but fated to be together, you're looking for the Devil card. If it comes out in the present or the future, the answer is a definite yes. If it doesn't come out, it probably means that they aren't, but that doesn't mean that they won't be a great couple together— or perhaps someday get married. Interpret the cards and leave yourself some room to understand what they're trying to tell you.

Here are a few other one-card quick "yes or no" examples to questions:

- Will I get pregnant in the next three months? The Empress card means motherhood and pregnancy.
- Can I trust him? The Seven of Swords is the betrayal card. If it comes out, it's an automatic no.
- Will I travel in the next three months? The Chariot always indicates travel, movement, and good news.
- Are we going to break up? The Ten of Swords is the heart breakup card, so getting this card in a reading is a definite yes.

These are just some examples of cards you can be on the lookout for—you'll learn others as you go along.

FACT

The same method will apply to reading tealeaves, runes, crystals, numerology, and other tools of divination. If you know what you're looking for after the question is asked and before you roll the dice, it makes it a whole lot easier. Plus, you'll know for sure that your reading is on the mark.

Recognizing Patterns

After doing a number of readings, you'll notice that certain symbols appear all the time. Take note of them. Perhaps they have a different meaning regarding a certain person. Or maybe they are trying to tell you something.

For instance, let's say you're doing a reading for your friend Mark. He's asking many questions about his work. For some reason, the Seven of Cups keeps popping up. Are the cards trying to tell him something? Though he hasn't asked anything specific that would relate back to the Seven of Cups, maybe there's something else going on that he's not aware of. The Seven of Cups can mean a few things: choices must be made; all that glitters is not gold; things are not as they seem. Is it coming up near a Queen or a King? Maybe there is someone at work who is being false with him and criticizes him behind his back. Or maybe he is avoiding making a decision that needs to be made.

Divination tools will speak to you. If Mark keeps talking about work but love cards keep coming out, perhaps his subconscious is communicating with and connecting with the energy. Advise him to ask a few questions regarding love. Watch out for and recognize the patterns that frequently appear. It will help you know you're on the right track.

Get Feedback

One of the most precious gifts you'll get is feedback, so listen up. If you do a reading for a friend and five months later she tells you that everything you told her was true, you know you're predicting with accuracy. If, on the other hand, she tells you that "this" and "that" was correct, but something else wasn't, take note. Are you better at predicting love than career? Are you better at long-term or short-term predictions?

In the beginning, feedback will be your best way of knowing if your predictions were accurate. It will also help you pinpoint the areas you need to work on. When you get feedback, accept it and decide how you can use it to improve your readings. Constructive criticism can be difficult to digest, but keep in mind who's giving it to you. If your colleague is abrasive and likes to stir up trouble, don't put too much credence into what he says about a reading you did for him two months ago. If, on the other hand, you did a reading for the older married woman down the street (whom you respect) and she tells you something about your predictions, listen carefully. Your instincts will tell you when to sit up and pay attention and when to let it pass by the wayside.

Swiss psychologist and psychiatrist Carl Gustav Jung stated, "Intuition is not mere perception, or vision, but an active, creative process that puts into the object just as much as it takes out" (*Collective Works VI*).

Holding On to Your Energy

Some people dislike having others touch their cards, crystals, runes, and other divination tools. You need to determine how you feel about this. Are you sensitive or superstitious? Do you believe that negative and positive energy is transferred easily? Most psychics have strong opinions about it. Many of them keep extra sets of things to use when doing readings for others. They keep their personal deck or crystals near and prefer not to let anyone else touch them.

This might seem like a strange concept. Put simply, energy rubs off on personal objects, clothing, and even space. This is why psychometry, the tool of divination practiced by touching a personal effect, is so effective, and why some people avoid buying antique jewelry or clothing. Others who buy antique jewelry make sure to cleanse its energy.

FACT

One method of cleansing personal objects or space (or even your own aura) is called "smudging." It's an old Native American practice done by lighting herbs and letting the smoke "heal" the negative energy. Today, smudging is done with a bundle of sage, cedar, lavender, sweetgrass, or tobacco.

Some people believe that there is no need for the person whose fortune is read to touch any of the divination tools the psychic is using. If you're the one reading, you're the one with whom the energy has to connect. Still others say this isn't true. They believe that the energy needs to flow through the querent to get a good reading, and they don't mind giving people their pack of cards to hold and shuffle. There is no right or wrong. Decide what's right for you.

Chapter 3

Omens and Signs in Everyday Life

Our lives are full of symbols that we refer to as a culture (like the American flag) or as individuals (your grandmother's special good-luck charm). Somehow, even if we're not looking for them, symbols, signs, and omens resurface again and again until we look up and take notice. In this chapter you'll learn how to pay attention when the universe is trying to tell you something!

Trust Your Instinct and Read the Signs

Even if you silence your intuition and ignore the signs around you, eventually you'll notice them—the signs and omens are everywhere. Omens, too, foretell good fortune or warn us of impending danger.

Did you ever meet someone and get an immediate feeling about her, whether it was a bad feeling or a good one? Or maybe something within told you not to trust that person? Did you go with your first impression or did you ignore it? What happened later? Instinct is that gut feeling that tells you not to get too close to a person or that it's okay if you do. If you listen to your instinct, you can have an idea of what you're getting yourself into.

It's important not to confuse instinct with a sign. Have you ever found that every time you make an appointment to see a certain friend, something always happens to thwart your plans? You don't get a bad feeling about it—it just happens. The tire blows out on your car; the flight gets canceled due to bad weather; your friend's in-laws show up unexpectedly and he has to stay and play host. This is a sign. The universe is putting in its two cents. Maybe it has to do with the timing of events—perhaps you're not ready to meet up with this particular person. Other times it's keeping you away from suffering or misguided intentions— the "friend" is not really a friend after all.

Dogs are very sensitive to the true character of people. They gravitate toward people they immediately like. On the other hand, if they have a negative reaction to a person, they react by barking or moving away. Animals trust their instincts, but humans sometimes stifle those instincts and rely on rationalization. Sometimes, it's best to trust your instinct, even if you have no logical explanation.

A Sign You Can't Ignore

Here is an example of how a woman discovered the hidden agenda of a "friend" purely by accident. Karen had an old friend from high school, Julia. One day, Julia came to her to ask for money, which she said she needed to pay rent and bills that were piling up. Karen was happy to help her friend. She gave Julia a large sum, which Julia promised to pay back when she got enough money together.

A few weeks later, Karen was window-shopping on the other side of town. One lovely jewelry store caught her eye and she went in. Strangely enough, the owner was another woman she had gone to high school with, but Karen hadn't seen her in fifteen years. Even stranger was the fact that the woman, upon seeing her, exclaimed: "Karen! It's so nice to see you after all this time! Are you still friends with Julia? She was in here last week and practically bought out the store. Do you still keep in touch?"

It turned out that Julia had spent Karen's money buying jewelry (Karen even saw Julia's signature in the sales book). Understandably, Karen was horrified. By a weird coincidence, she had discovered what her friend's emergency really was—a shopping spree! Finding out that Julia had deceived her was a big shock, but she decided to give her the benefit of the doubt. When she approached Julia about it, Julia denied everything. At that point Karen knew the friendship was really over. Who wants a friend you can't trust?

Perhaps there were other signs before this incident pointing to the true character of her friend, but Karen had ignored them. This time she had no choice but to take notice. Karen let go and moved on. Has something like this ever happened to you?

Is It for Real?

If you're looking for a particular sign, most likely you'll find it. But that doesn't mean it's a real sign. In fact, if you're really looking for anything, you're bound to see it in many places. This kind of thinking can be dangerous. Did it ever seem that after you've had a big breakup, every radio station is playing more love songs? They're not. You're just noticing it more because it applies to your state of mind.

ALERT!

Don't go looking for signs—they're supposed to come to you. You have a life to live, remember? So the big question is, should we relate every strange occurrence in our lives back to destiny? Should we believe that every glitch in life is a sign of fate? Of course not. Signs exist everywhere, but you can't run your life well by looking for them everywhere you go.

A Meaningful Coincidence

Coincidences do often carry meaning and power. Here is a story to illustrate this point. Andrew had just come back from a trip to Paris and was out for a walk with his friend Lauren. "I'm thinking about moving there," he confided to her.

Lauren encouraged him. She told him that if he wanted to move to Europe, Paris would be a wonderful place for him. As they walked, they discussed where he might live, his career choices, and what it would be like to be away from friends and family. Andrew wasn't sure if it was a good move.

Then, something shiny caught his eye on the street. He reached down and picked it up. It was a miniature key-chain model of the Eiffel tower—right there on Fifty-third Street in New York City. He stared at it, showed it to his friend, and started laughing. How incredible. Was it a "sign" or merely a coincidence? How can you tell the difference?

Recognizing Patterns

It's not easy to tell the difference. Some people will also tell you that there is no such thing as coincidence. Who's to say they're not right? One good way to decide whether the coincidence is real or not is this: Has it happened more than once?

Signs of the universe come in patterns. A coincidence of the same genre might happen again and again until you finally "get it." At that point, whether or not you act on it is your decision. Sometimes you have no choice—the universe pushes it in your face and decides for you. The signs are only there to provide you with the opportunity to learn and to change. If you use them to your advantage, it can make life a whole lot easier.

Let's take another example. You've worked as a tax accountant your entire life but your big dream is to be a professional photographer. And for some bizarre reason, everywhere you go strangers are always picking you out of a group to take their picture. It doesn't matter where you are— across the street from your house or traveling in China—they hand you the camera and give you directions for how they'd like their picture taken, please. The first few times it happens you're flattered. But after a while, it becomes more than just coincidence. Truth be told, this is not a coincidence, but a sign. Things that happen over and over again until you notice them are the world's way of speaking to you. Coincidences are its way to really get you to start paying attention.

Another Scenario

Does it ever happen that you keep running into the same person over and over again? Perhaps it's someone you only know by sight or with whom you've had a few conversations. But somehow they always seem to have the same agenda you have. Strangely enough, you see them at the hairdresser's and then later at the supermarket, and then you see them on the other side of town. It could be that this person has some information for you. If you keep seeing someone constantly, take a moment and think—is there meaning behind it? Similar coincidences over time are trying to tell you something. Maybe you should dig deeper and explore what that person may have to tell you.

When a Coincidence Is a Sign

Here's another example of coincidence. Your mother keeps trying to set you up with her friend's daughter, but a blind date is the last thing on your mind. You tell her you don't do blind dates, but she's offended and you feel guilty.

UESTION?

Is there such a thing as a soul mate?
There is, absolutely. Actually, many psychics say that there is no such thing as just one soul mate—we all have a few of them we'll meet in our lifetime. It is said that very few people are destined to marry a soul mate.

One night you're out with friends, and one of them tells you that he wants you to meet a friend of his. It turns out that it's the same woman with whom your mother has been trying to set you up. You wonder if it's a coincidence. Not a chance.

But this does not necessarily mean that she was meant for you. In fact, it's more likely that you're meant to learn a lesson from your interaction with her. Or perhaps it's the universe's way of showing you what you don't want, so you'll know what you do want when you stumble on it. It could also be that she is a possible career contact, even in a roundabout way. In any case, you'll be prodded and poked until you meet her. These kinds of things happen for a reason. Sometimes we only find out what that reason is later on. What do you believe?

Miracles and Superstitions

Miracles may be big or small, everyday or historic, related to matters of faith or spirituality. You read about them every day: The child in a car wreck who walks away unscathed, the man who has three months to live and suddenly recovers and is given a clean bill of health. These events cannot be explained by science. They're miracles, they're beautiful, and they've existed throughout time.

Miracles Explained

Can you ask for a miracle? Of course you can. But miracles happen with or without asking. Many people are convinced that if they want something badly enough, and pray for it, it will happen, but no one knows for sure how this works. Some people even claim that they saved themselves from certain death through prayer and visualization. In any case, asking the universe to grant you something you need can do no harm. The best thing you can do to make it happen is to put yourself in a position (a good state of mind) where the gift can reach you.

ALERT!

Your body is very sensitive to the suggestions of the subconscious mind. This means that if you fear something enough, it can manifest itself through very real physical symptoms.

Are You Superstitious?

Superstitions have also been around for as long as mankind has walked the earth. They were originally created out of fear and ignorance. Many of us still use them today, though more out of habit than of trepidation. Many universal superstitions originated from the belief in evil spirits—the concept that something bad will happen to you if you don't ward off the evil by steps like knocking on wood or throwing salt over your left shoulder.

Some superstitions are so common that we don't even notice them anymore. For example, saying "God bless you" when a person sneezes these days is simply a polite thing to do. The tradition, though, started hundreds of years ago, when many believed that the devil could enter your body while you sneezed. "God bless you" was a phrase said to drive the devil away.

FACT

Throwing salt over your shoulder is an old superstition considered to ward off bad luck and evil spirits. It is said that when you spill the salt, you must immediately throw more salt over your left shoulder—into the devil's face.

In addition to cultural superstitions, each person has a few superstitions of her own. For example, if you don't use a certain pillow at night, do you have trouble sleeping? Do you ever take just one more candy because it feels right (or it evened out the number of them), and not because you want more? Do you ever hang up a coat on the same hanger because it "belongs" there? Superstitions we create do nothing but serve and feed our need for them, but also it's possible that they make our lives a little more interesting.

Weird but True—Superstitions Revealed

Here is a list of superstitions, from the most common to the downright strange.

- If you make a wish on a shooting star, your wish will come true.
- When you hear a bell ringing, it means an angel has received its wings.
- A rabbit's foot worn on your person will protect you from misfortune.
- You should never leave an empty rocking chair rocking because it invites evil spirits into your house.
- If you break a mirror, you'll have seven years of bad luck.
- If you pick up a coin off the ground and it's "heads," you'll have good luck.
- If you pull out a gray hair, ten more will pop up as a result.
- A statue of an elephant placed in the house will bring good luck, but only if the trunk faces up.
- If your ear itches, someone is talking about you.

There are literally thousands of superstitions out there—and they involve everything from not walking under a ladder to never killing a ladybug. Which ones did you grow up with?

ALERT!

Did you ever hear about a singer who lost her voice right before a big concert? Have you ever started a new gym routine, determined to get into shape, and wound up with a sprained ankle? On your first day of high school, were you the one with a pimple right on the tip of your nose? Embrace your fears and conquer them before they can get to you. If you don't, your fear will find you.

A Prophetic Sign

Some signs that predict the coming of certain events in life are known as omens. Omens may be good or bad, personal or universal. They have existed in nature since ancient times: flight patterns of birds signify the coming of storms; seeing the stars clearly tonight portends a beautiful, sunny day tomorrow. Native American cultures have always let natural omens guide them in everything they do in life—when to plant crops, when to hunt, when to bear children.

All superstitions were originally omens; when an omen becomes widely known and feared (or outdated), it is labeled as a superstition. A black cat crossing your path was an omen of bad luck; now the belief that the cat will bring you bad luck is called a superstition.

Letting It Happen

You are the maker of your destiny. But there are some things in life you can't control. If something simply wasn't meant to be, there's nothing you can do about it. Many psychics who do a reading for you can usually see in the cards, for example, if the person you're with right now is the one you'll stay with or marry. Some won't tell you this unless you ask them directly.

Why don't they say anything? Because there's nothing you can do about it and they know it. Sooner or later it will happen, whether you want it to or not. And since there's nothing you can do to change it, why not just enjoy the ride? If your fantasy is to sing the national anthem at the next big game, and a fairy granted your wish but told you your voice would crack when you reach the really high notes, wouldn't you do it anyway?

It's All about Options

Your job as a reader is not necessarily to protect the querent from his destiny. You only need to read what you see. You should give the querent advice and options and then let him find his way for himself. Remind the person you're reading for that everything you see in the future hinges on the way he handles himself. Until issues and conflicts are resolved within, the same problems in life will keep resurfacing until he does something about it. But if he's meant to learn this life lesson, no amount of advice or prediction through divination will help him change the inevitable.

People who get addicted to divination—who run to psychics every other week—are looking for answers that don't exist. If you have a feeling that the path you're on is the wrong one but you still stay on it for a while, that's okay. Sometimes it takes time for us to accept the fact that no matter how hard we try, not everything in our lives will go according to plan. But if you are trying to manipulate the outcome of an event, remember that all that glitters is not gold. What you may think you want might not be a good thing for you at all.

Take Action!

The universe pushes and prods you to do things. You can pretend that you don't see the little hints for your entire life and, all at once, it'll hit you between the eyes. Did you ever notice, for example, that people who hate being alone always wind up with the wrong person? They never wait for the right one to come along. Instead, they go in and out of relationships, never stopping a minute to think why none of their relationships work out. Deep down, they know they're a little needy and they should try being on their own for a while, but they avoid it at all costs. Why? Self-preservation: They don't think they can handle it.

Eventually, though, if they don't take action on their own, the world will throw them for a loop when they're not expecting it. And it will be a tough one. All of a sudden, they're forced to deal with painful issues—and they're not prepared for it. The truth is, none of us wants to be responsible for things over which we really have no control. So we complain about life and how unfair it is. True, the universe puts us in some pretty difficult situations, but we also create difficult situations for ourselves. If you get a warning sign first, make a change and get going in the right direction—before things start getting hairy.

Many people don't understand that fear, depression, anxiety, and happiness are all subjective—they are how you *feel*, not how things actually are. Feelings are not facts; they are truths, your life as you choose to see it.

You can change your thought process simply by making up your mind to do it. If you decide you want to be happy, you can be happy. The same is true of signs and symbols of the universe. The number thirteen, for example, is considered to be bad luck in many cultures, but some people insist that it's good luck for them.

Take a Step Toward Change

The fact is, if you're reading this chapter right now, you're obviously looking to improve your life. Divination can help you do just that. If the divining tools are telling you something, you need to do something about it.

Be aware that the art of divination is there to guide you, not to provide a quick fix or two-cent advice. Did you ever meet someone who spends all her free time reading self-help books but has more problems than anyone else you know? This person spends a lot of time thinking about how she can improve herself and little time doing something about it. Don't get caught up in this kind of brain play. If you know you need to change your life in some way, don't procrastinate. Do something about it. It may save you from some unnecessary suffering down the line.

FACT

Lao-tzu (600 B.C.), the founder of Taoism, said: "A journey of a thousand miles must begin with a single step." In Chinese, *Tao* literally means "the way."

Don't Go Overboard!

Here's the kicker—not everything in life is a sign, symbol, or coincidence trying to tell you something. In fact, reality is merely what we perceive it is. Therefore, if you believe that every move you make is "watched" or "judged," you're really going to go off the deep end! Keep in mind that not everyone you meet is put in your life for a reason, and not everything boils down to fate. Things happen. It's life.

The way to stay grounded is this: Think of all those billions of people out there. They're all living their lives, too. It's kind of presumptuous for one person to think that everything out there happens because it relates back to his own destiny. Certainly, the airline company losing lots of money by canceling a flight due to weather conditions wouldn't agree that it came about as part of your personal fate.

Ego sometimes makes us think that the world revolves around us. We tend to play mind tricks on ourselves, though we don't realize it at the time. And we frequently entertain the notion that we actually have influence over the things that happen around us, whereas most of the time we don't. It all comes down to that intangible thing we all crave and desperately search to have: control. By giving up a part of that control and not looking for signs everywhere in life, we live our lives better and stay mentally in the here and now.

Perhaps divination interests you more at this time in your life because you're having a rough moment. Take heart. It may sometimes seem that difficult situations are constantly landing only in your lap, but everyone has felt that way at one time or another.

When we're learning about life signs, coincidences, and forms of divination, it's common to go a bit overboard at first. It's exciting, new, fresh information. And when you digest all of the facts out there and realize that psychic phenomena and universal energy really exist, you can't help but be hooked. Just remember one thing: It's not good to know too much information about your future. Because of free will, we can change things easily. And when you learn beforehand your fate and your destiny, it makes you lazy—you stop working toward your goals. You take everything for granted. And this changes your future. Keep living your life the way you were living it before. Don't get too involved.

The great masters agree—we are all a part of a greater force. The key is to tap into that force and become one small but important piece of the bigger whole. If you're just learning divination, think of it in the same way. It's a small part of learning more about yourself and the people around you. Don't go off the deep end. Take it slowly and you'll eventually begin to understand the bigger plan. Ⓔ

Chapter 4

Timing Is Everything

Being successful in divination requires good timing. Of course, there really is no right or wrong time to look into your future, as long as you feel that the time you've chosen is right for you. Still, if you become familiar with the way the mechanics of the world affect your energy and intuition, you can improve the accuracy of your predictions. In this chapter, you'll see how closely time and energy are linked and find out how this knowledge can strengthen your intuitive powers.

In Tune with the Rhythms of Life

Every second in life is unique unto itself because it will never be repeated again. You can never go back in time, however much you may wish to do so. How many times have we heard someone say, "the timing was off," or "we've run out of time"? Timing is so important in every aspect in our lives, and yet most of us take it for granted.

We're influenced by more than just the hours of the day. The seasons, the months, the years, the day length are regulated by the sun, and the cycles of the moon all play an important role in our everyday lives. These time periods are said to move in rhythms, phases, cycles, waves, and other esoteric equations that are so complex it could make your head spin.

The modern world is ruled by clocks. We don't watch the stars in order to determine how we should proceed; we hardly pay attention to the change of seasons. But prehistoric humans did. They planned hunting, farming, and sacred feasts according to the cycles of time. The ancient cultures made prophecies and predictions according to the reports of sky watchers, those who followed the positions of the sun, the moon, and the stars, as well as appearances of comets and solar eclipses.

FACT

Since ancient times, the stars and the planets have had so much importance in our lives that many words in our language have to do with a particular star or planet. For example, the word "lunatic," which refers to a person who acts in a crazy manner, came from the Latin word *luna* (moon).

We are the universe and the universe is us. We are all part of a bigger picture and we're influenced by what goes on around us. Our energy, our powers of intuition, and our moods are all affected by the movements of the universe. Therefore, when we're practicing divination, we need to take a good look at the workings of the universe in order to get our timing right. The days of the week, as well as the cycles of the moon, the sun, and the stars, have the power to enhance or weaken your powers of divination.

Cycles of Time and Space

Everything in nature moves in cycles. Each living thing is born, grows, ages, and eventually dies. The tides have cycles. The moon's influence on Earth is cyclic. The seasons change year after year in cycles. Women have their own menstrual cycles, and men have hormonal cycles. Even in wars, fashion, music, wildlife, and the economy, cycles are evident and inevitable. Everything in the world is cyclic, and has its own rhythm, force, vibration, wave, pattern, and time frame.

ALERT!

Every life form has its own estimated time period on this planet. A dog's life cycle, for example, is measured by figuring seven human years to one canine year. Therefore, a ten-year-old dog is considered to be equivalent in age to a seventy-year-old person.

Why is this information about cycles so important? Well, in divination you're gathering and harnessing the energy around you. And since the beginning of time, we have searched for a way to define and analyze this intangible entity. Energy runs in cycles, too: it ebbs, flows, intensifies, and diminishes. And it's necessary to be aware of the changeability of energy when you're tapping into your psychic self. Your intuitive state, your moods, your emotions, and your creativity all get stronger and diminish along with this cycle of energy. And all of these things will affect your readings—giving and getting them.

Determining Cycles

Which cycles will affect you the most? There are many to consider.

- **Moon cycles:** These are the cycles you'll have to pay attention to more than the others. The moon strongly influences your energy. It takes 27½ days for the moon's cycle to complete itself and, in between, there is the full moon, the waning moon, the waxing moon, and the new moon. The moon will give you most energy when it is in your sun sign and also during a full moon, which boosts creativity and emotionally charged reactions.

- **Sun cycles:** One cycle of the sun—that is, the earth's rotation around the sun—is completed in 365¼ days. Your health, intuition, and personal energy are all affected by sun cycles. The best time to give or get a reading is on or near your birthday, when your energy is the strongest. Six months later, your energy may be at its lowest. It's better if you don't get a reading then unless there is a full moon.

- **Days of the week:** From Monday to Sunday, each day of the week has specific energies attached to it. Questions concerning career, love, health, or leisure should be asked depending on the days of the week and their power properties, which we'll get to a little later.

- **Depression and anxiety:** Our crisis phases come at different points in each person's life. Many times we experience a period of suffering (including denial, anger, and, finally, acceptance). Though we may want to look to divination to help guide us through these times, it is actually not the best time to give or get a reading. When you feel yourself coming out of it, go for a reading and explore your opportunities. It will help you move on to the next mode.

- **Death and rebirth:** After a major turning point in our lives, a small part of us dies and is replaced by new energy, a new force. The cycle of death and rebirth is necessary so that we may change and evolve. During the year following this cycle, your intuition is increased and you're more sensitive to the energy around you. It's a good idea to give readings during this period.

- **Seven-year cycle:** Did you ever hear of the seven-year itch? Many spiritual leaders suggest that every seven years, we take stock of what's around us, throw out what's not working (whether in a career or a relationship), and bring in the new. For three months before and after this seven-year point, getting a reading helps you to evaluate your life options.

A woman's menstrual cycle is usually twenty-eight days—just like the cycle of the moon. Is it a coincidence? We don't know. Scientists have established that the moon influences the ocean tides. Could it also influence the female body? It's possible!

Saturn Return

Each of us will experience a Saturn Return approximately every thirty years. A Saturn Return is when the planet Saturn completes its cycle through your birth chart and returns back to the spot where it was at the time when you were born. For the last two years of this thirty-year interval, you will experience an intense period of change, enlightenment, or crisis, depending on what you've done with your life up until that point. So, your Saturn Return will accost you at the ages between twenty-eight and thirty, fifty-eight and sixty, and eighty-eight and ninety (though most of us have got it down by then). Few people describe this phase as pleasant. Normally, the terms "difficult and challenging" come to mind.

The time of the Saturn Return requires us to take a better look at the big picture and make radical adjustments in our life. When it arrives, it brings changes to our attitudes, lifestyles, and relationships with ourselves and with others. This is a good time to get a reading as well as to read for others.

For Women Only

It's taken a long time for women to realize that the menstrual cycle, which takes about twenty-eight days, is a cycle of wonder, power, strength, change, and movement. What does the menstrual cycle have to do with divination? Besides the inconvenience, the cramps, and the PMS, a woman can claim certain benefits from menstruation. It's a time of heightened awareness—her intuition sharpens, she becomes more defined with her likes and dislikes, and her emotional states become more intensified. She is more aware of all of her senses: touch, hearing, smell, vision, and taste.

Three days before her menstrual period and up to five days after it commences is the time when a woman gets that extra boost from the universe. Although she may not feel like it, the best time for a woman to give readings is during these eight or nine days. Also, it may sound a little wacky, but if there is a full moon during this period, her intuition is increased tenfold. This is also an excellent time for her to do readings for herself, if she so desires.

Establish Your Own Cycles

The best way to figure out which cycles influence you most is to keep a diary or a journal. By noting the highs and lows of your days and your weeks, you will be able to recognize your own spiritual energy pattern. Every person has a distinct energy vibration that changes and flows according to your life plan.

Luck and intuition are closely linked. What may sometimes feel like luck can actually be your intuition kicked into high gear. If you're playing blackjack, for example, and you're winning nearly every hand, is it because you're going with your gut? If the answer is yes, chances are it's thanks to your intuition.

You don't even have to write down what you do or whom you see. Extra details can help you, but they aren't necessary. If you want, keep a little calendar next to your bed. At the end of the day, rate your energy level from 1 to 30. Note that this has nothing to do with how tired you are or if you happen to be sick. Even if you don't sleep at all, you can still sense whether your spiritual energy level is high and whether you're in a positive cycle. After that, rate your luck level on the same scale. You should have something that looks like this:

Date	Energy	Luck
Monday, June 28	15	19
Tuesday, June 29	12	21
Wednesday, June 30	17	3

After doing it for a while, perhaps seven or eight months, you should see a pattern. When your energy is high, it's a good time to get a reading. If your luck is high, it also means your intuition is up and it's the best time to give a reading.

Repeating Mistakes

Have you ever gotten yourself into a sticky situation but then managed to get yourself out of it by sheer dumb luck? Maybe you told a little white lie. Nobody found out and so you resumed your life with or without guilt pangs. And then you found yourself in that same situation again. Perhaps this time the little white lie was an even bigger white lie. And this time, you're found out. Didn't you learn your lesson the first time?

Actually, no, you didn't. Aside from karma, action and reaction, and maybe even a need for self-torment, why do we make the same mistakes again? Well, the universe has its time frames, its cycles. When you get stuck in a rut, it's as if the universe's record is skipping and returning back to the same point. How do you get out of it? What do you need to do? Well obviously, you're doing something wrong. Possibly, there is a different way you need to handle your affairs. It's probable, too, that the problem has nothing to do with the situation that keeps repeating. This is just a small symptom of the bigger bug.

Tuning In to the Problem

If the universe is trying to tell you something, it's a good idea to give yourself a reading (or find someone else to do it for you) and meditate over your possibilities. You're at a turning point in your life and for you to move forward, something needs to give. Divination can tell you what that something is.

ALERT!

Take heart! Deep suffering for a lost relationship or the loss of someone who was close to you is a clear sign that you are nearing a crucial turning point in your life. When one door closes another one opens, but it only opens when you're ready for it. The timing is up to you. When you're ready to let go, the difficult period will pass.

The Days of the Week

You can perform divination any day of the week. If you've been keeping a journal, you might want to check to find if you have one day that happens to be lucky for you. Additionally, each day is favorable for a particular kind of reading. If you have questions focusing on a particular area, here is the list of days to help you choose the most favorable one:

1. **Monday, the day of the moon.** Ask questions regarding home, pregnancy, children, obsessions, and hidden emotions and intentions.
2. **Tuesday, the day of the planet Mars.** Ask questions regarding travel, fortitude, short-term relationships, and sex.
3. **Wednesday, the day of Mercury.** Ask questions regarding career, communication, long-distance friendships and relationships, and future goals.
4. **Thursday, the day of Jupiter.** Ask questions regarding money, financial issues, and contracts.
5. **Friday, the day of Venus.** Ask questions regarding love, home, romance, and friendships.
6. **Saturday, the day of Saturn.** Ask questions regarding work, projects, obstacles, finding stability, and any issues regarding trust.
7. **Sunday, the day of the sun.** Ask general questions.

During the year, other good days to practice divination are all holidays (especially All Hallows' Eve—Halloween) and the first day of each of the seasons.

Reading According to Your Sun Sign

Do you know your sun sign? If you do, it can help you pick a good day of the week for divining. Here are the days of the week that are good divining days for you:

- **Aries:** Tuesday
- **Taurus:** Saturday
- **Gemini:** Thursday and Friday

- **Cancer:** Monday and Tuesday
- **Leo**: Sunday and Thursday
- **Virgo:** Tuesday
- **Libra:** Friday
- **Scorpio:** Friday and Saturday
- **Sagittarius:** Thursday
- **Capricorn:** Saturday
- **Aquarius:** Sunday and Monday
- **Pisces:** Wednesday

Phases of the Moon

There are four phases of the moon: the new moon, the full moon, the waxing moon, and the waning moon. Each one of them has a direct effect on your energy and intuition. To find out which phase the moon is in, all you need to do is go outside.

Look at the moon tonight. If you see the crescent with the tips pointing to the left, the moon is "waxing" or becoming full. When the tips of the moon are pointing to the right, it is "waning" or disappearing.

▲ Moon phases: New, waxing, full, and waning moon.

The New Moon

Divination done during the new moon is very powerful. The phase perfect for this is three days before the new moon to three days after. Questions about projects or relationships recently started or just ending are perfect subjects to bring up at this time. Some people say that the best time to perform divination with the new moon is during the daytime. You can also ask questions focused on health, beauty, creative endeavors, money, legal matters, jobs, love, and romance. Analyze the significance of certain dreams you have at this time.

FACT

The moon has always fascinated human beings, and folkloric beliefs regarding the moon abound. Many ancient cultures believed that it was bad luck if a new moon fell on a Monday. Sailors predicted that a storm was coming if they could see a large star close to the moon. And here's a custom for getting a love wish to come true—spend an hour staring at the moon, reciting your wish out loud.

The Full Moon

Hands down, this is the best phase of the moon to practice divination. For seven days—three days before and three days after the full moon, and the day the full moon occurs—you'll reap the benefits of the dazzling energy that the moon gives out. Your intuition and psychic vision will be incredibly enhanced during this period. You will also be more sensitive and emotional. This is a great time to ask questions about family, love, motivations of others, competition, money, fitness and health, decisions, pregnancy and children, and self-improvement. Dreams of a prophetic nature tend to occur during this phase of the moon cycle. You can also ask the moon for protection and guidance during this time.

The Waning Moon

When the moon is disappearing or "waning," it is changing from full moon to new moon. Some people prefer not to practice divination during this period, which starts after the fourth day of the actual day of the full moon and lasts for seven days. If you need to ask questions at this time, you can try inquiring about addictions, stress, debts, issues of trust, and emotional blocks.

The Waxing Moon

The waxing moon period is when the moon is increasing in size, from new or black back to full. At this time, your energy and strength increase as well. It is best to do divination after the fourth day of the actual new moon. You can ask all questions of a positive nature, as well as advice on how to handle things. You can also focus on friends, how people feel about you, luck, and travel.

The Moon in Your Sun Sign

To keep track of when the moon is in your sun sign, you can find astrological calendars online or purchase *The World Almanac,* which contains this information. When the moon is in your sun sign, it's a good time to ask questions concerning advice, decisions, and just about anything in general. Luck and intuition are on your side, and your energy is stronger as well, so you can go ahead and get a reading during this period. If the moon is in your sign and it is full, your chances for accuracy are greatly increased.

Why the Future Didn't Come True

In divination, it's very difficult to predict the exact timing of an event. If something didn't happen the way the cards foretold it, there are four possible explanations for it. The first one has to do with real destiny and free will, but the other three (explained in following sections) have to do with timing.

Only a few things in your life are going to happen whether you want them to or not. This is fate, real destiny. Because of free will, and because of choices you made along the way, a job you plan on getting might not come through. If this happens, think of it as a blip, an inconsequential event that has no real bearing on your life plan. You may not think of it this way at the moment, but just wait and see. The universe would have seen to it that you got the job if it was meant to further your life plan. It's possible you're not ready for it.

It's Not Your Time

How many times have you heard this? Did it make you angry? It's a common sentiment. But unfortunately, the statement makes sense—it's the way things work. The universe forces us to deal with obstacles in order to make us stronger and to help us prepare for the next level.

If your predictions are off the mark in divination, it's very possible that your questions are too general. Instead of asking, "Will I get the job?" try asking more specialized questions that have specific answers, such as "Now that I've had my interview, should I make a follow-up call?" or "Is this job part of my life plan?"

It's Hard to Tell When

Understanding the timing and the sequence of events in divination can be challenging. Even seasoned experts can have a tough time of it. As you go along, you'll get a better idea of relative time frames. With Tarot readings, for example, some people interpret different suits as referring to different time periods: Cups represent days, Wands weeks, Swords months, and Pentacles years. Others say it's an issue best left up to instinct. In astrology and numerology, dates and time periods can be more specifically pinpointed.

The interesting thing about divination tools is that sometimes you can ask a specific question and the answer you'll receive is actually referring to another question—one that hasn't been asked yet! Why? Because when you're divining the future, you're asking for help and guidance. If you go into it with a good attitude, you'll get the guidance you need. In fact, if you're constantly asking questions of no consequence to your future, the divination tool you're using will start nudging you in a different direction. Consequently, you might start getting answers to the questions you're supposed to ask.

For example, if you keep asking about work and career but only relationship cards keep coming up, the cards are trying to tell you something about someone close to you. Perhaps this person is a contact you'll need to get a break at work. Or maybe something about your relationship with this person is holding you back from getting ahead in your career.

Also, when the cards told you that you'd get the job, are you sure they were referring to this particular job? Or are they clueing you in to a different one—possibly one you don't know about yet? Ask more questions. It's probable that there is something you need to do in order to open the door for new work leads.

Be Aware of the Time Frame

There are time frames, or windows, that stay open only for a specific period of time. If you ask direct questions about what to do in a certain situation, I Ching and the Tarot cards will give you direct answers (either to act now or to wait because it's not the time yet). Asking guidance about the time frame is incredibly important. You need to know when to move on a certain issue, or you might miss out on a good opportunity.

Chapter 5

Setting the Mood

It's essential to set the mood before a reading. No psychic worth his salt is going to plop down in a chair, whip out a deck of cards, and start a reading. He always makes the necessary preparations first. When you're divining, you're calling on the positive spiritual energy surrounding you. The ritual of setting the mood is a sort of meditation that requires you to focus, define your goals and intentions, and open your mind to the universe.

Light the Candles

Why are candles used so often with divination? Because they work. You can use candles in prayer, for "magick" (the spiritual manipulation of energy, not to be confused with "magic"), and for wishes. They are also wonderful for cleansing and harnessing energy. Since the beginning of time, smoke and fire were considered to be tools of awesome power. They were used for protection and survival and united man with the Earth and the universe. All ancient cultures believed this, no matter how varied their other philosophies were.

FACT

Aleister Crowley, creator of one of the decks of the Tarot, said, "Indubitably, 'Magick' is one of the subtlest and most difficult of the sciences and arts. There is more opportunity for errors of comprehension, judgment, and practice than in any other branch of physics."

Because fire is pure, candles attract and give off only positive energy. And since fire cleanses, candles can also purify negative energy. Candles affect your mental state as well. You know that aromatherapy (healing by the power of scents) works so well with candles. Even a candle without a particular scent has the power to influence you. The smell of smoke can also evoke your spirituality, memories, intuition, and deep emotions—all attributes you rely on in divination.

Divination Candles

Each candle you use for divination should have its own specific purpose. For example, you should have one candle for when you read for others and another candle for when you read for yourself. Make sure to use a different candle for the sole purpose of making wishes or, perhaps, one for placing at your dinner table. Each candle should have its own function. Don't, for example, use your dinner candle for divination. When you are about to do a reading, be sure that you are the one lighting the divination candle; after you are done, make sure you snuff it out.

If you have guests over for dinner, you can guide the energy (and the conversation) with the help of candles. Choose an orange candle if you'd like to liven things up and let conversation flow. Blue is to bring calm to the gathering. For a romantic dinner, get pink, white, or red (if you want to ignite the passion). Brown will balance the energy. Purple will add a little strangeness.

Choosing a Candle

You'll want to stay away from candles with many different colors and patterns. Choose a candle of one solid color, because colors vibrate at different frequencies and are used for tapping into different energies. Here is a list of the colors and their applications in prayer, magick, and divination:

- **White:** This color encompasses all the other colors of the spectrum and is said to be able to harness the power of the moon. White candles should be used in accordance with moon phases. Use them for peace and purity, truth-seeking, cleansing and healing, accessing spirituality and intuition, and divination.
- **Red:** Linked with the planet Mars, red is the color of passion and short-term adventures and events. People with the sun signs of Aries or Scorpio can use this candle to fuel up on good energy. In prayer and in magick, red is also used for courage, strength, fire, lust, and health. You should generally avoid using red candles in divination, except in rare cases (for example, for a flirt or a short-term adventure, not for marriage, children, or anything long-term).
- **Yellow and gold:** These colors draw energy from the sun. Use yellow and gold candles for confidence, inspiration, creativity, and memory. They are especially lucky for those who have their sun sign in Leo. In magick and prayer, these colors are good for persuasion (influences over other people, career, and health). You can also use pale yellow candles for divination.
- **Pink:** The color of Venus, pink is associated with romantic love and affection. Pink candles can help discover real intentions in friendship

and love. Pink is a good color for magick and for wishes, prayer, and divination. It helps to use it in accordance with the full and new phases of the moon.

- **Purple:** These candles are used for psychic strength, but you can't rely on them too often, as this color is very powerful and requires a lot of energy. Purple is associated with spiritual and psychic ability, ambition, and independence. Sagittarians are influenced by this color. You can use purple in magick and prayer for important business and legal matters; it brings luck. In divination, use only for questions of paramount importance.

- **Black:** This color, related to Saturn, is good for candles used for cleansing. Together, white and black candles work to cancel out bad energy. Use black first, then white. Black also releases sadness and pain. It pushes away negative vibrations. This candle is used for prayer and sometimes in magick. It is rarely used in divination. This is a good color for Capricorns.

- **Orange:** This color uses the powers of Mercury and the Sun. It's a good color for luck, success, writing and communication, smooth business transactions, attraction, and solidifying friendships. An orange candle helps alleviate tension and bad moods. You can use it both in magick and in divination.

- **Green:** The color of abundance, it's good to use for harmony, peace, and luck in financial matters. For women, fertility and pregnancy can be wished for and predicted with a green candle. You can use green candles in prayer, magick, and financial/fertility questions in divination.

- **Blue:** Associated with Neptune and Jupiter, blue is used in meditation for its properties of soothing and bringing calmness and peace. You can also use it for understanding emotions and thoughts; generally, blue brings truth and higher wisdom. Blue and green candles both are good for Pisces. Use a blue candle for prayer and divination.

- **Brown:** This color is connected with the earth. It can help you make decisions and attract security. Don't use this color for questions or prayer concerning people. It's better to use this candle in meditation.

ALERT!

Candles work to attract certain energies when they're lit. But they also work when they're out! If you're using a candle for prayer or for attaining wishes, keep it out where you can see it. This way, you'll always benefit from the positive vibrations surrounding it.

Preparing Your Candle

Give the candle its own space. Make sure it's not surrounded by clutter and a mass of other objects. You'll want to give the candle some of your own vibrations. You can also rub the candle with some essential oil. Hold the candle in your left hand. Rub the candle from bottom to top and then down to the bottom again. Close your eyes and smile. Let your mind wander. Feel positive and think about your goals. Visualize success.

Now, hold the candle in the center with your right hand. Put it down. Light it (it's best to use a match, but a lighter will do). Then say: "Please give me strength, guidance, and wisdom. Thank you." Close your eyes and say a short prayer of thanks to whomever you're asking for help. Open your eyes. You're ready.

Relaxing Tunes

Music is so important for setting any mood. It shapes our feelings and hits us with its intensity. It evokes half-forgotten memories, dreams, and desires. It soothes the savage beast. It can either aid you or distract you when you're performing divination. You'll want to use music that helps you, not hinders you. But what kind of music suits looking into the future?

What You Should Avoid

First, let's look at which types of music you should not use for divination:

- **Songs with words.** You don't want to be distracted by phrases or meaning.

- **Music with excessive rhythm or percussion.** It can give an unwanted rhythm to the energy around you and may even cause anxiety.
- **Music from a certain era.** Ragtime, blues, and opera are all examples of music that has the tendency to send you back in time, not forward to the future.
- **Songs that evoke emotion.** A good reading requires that you remain objective, which will be difficult if you are emotionally affected by the music.
- **Pop music.** If you can hum along to a song or expect a cadence before it's coming, you know the song too well and it will distract you.
- **Anything loud.** Music should be unobtrusive, not overwhelming.

The goal is to be relaxed. If certain music on this list of "don'ts" helps you to unwind, try playing it before your reading, as a sort of warm-up.

QUESTION?

Why is it better, for the purposes of divination, to stay away from songs that evoke my emotions?
Music brings out deep-seated memories and old childhood neuroses, and divination tools pick them up, affecting your answers. You don't want your reading to be influenced in the process.

Better Options

Here are the kinds of music and background sounds that are good for divination:

- **Inspirational music.** Tunes of inspiration are good, as long as you keep it simple.
- **Songs that don't feature a singer or one musical instrument.** An orchestra or a group of instruments are less likely to affect your mood.

- **Repetitive music or chants.** If the music is the same over and over, it's easier to block out and will help you to focus on the reading at hand.
- **Background sounds.** Sounds like "running brook," "wildlife," and "waterfall" can be very soothing. Water sounds can be especially helpful for creating a serene ambiance.
- **Calming music.** Use anything tranquil or peaceful, as long as it doesn't stir emotions.
- **Music of another culture.** It doesn't matter if the music has singing, since you can't understand what the singer is saying. And because it's in a foreign language, it won't attract your attention as much.

Relying on Feng Shui

While you're setting the mood, why not maximize the energy of your surroundings? According to the ancient Chinese teachings of feng shui, even the little things you change around your house can help bring you luck, inspiration, and positive energy.

Feng shui (pronounced "fung shway") teaches that we must live in harmony with our environment. If we do this, we will live a happy, fulfilled life. Literally, feng shui means "wind and water." The Chinese believed that if you could balance these elements in your life (for example, in your home), you would attract fortune and prosperity. They named this universal life force *ch'i*.

The Key to Ch'i

Ch'i (pronounced "chee") is what the ancient Chinese called "the dragon's cosmic breath," the energy and universal power that governs the world. Ch'i is present everywhere and is in constant flux. It moves, flows, and pools in certain areas inside and outside your home. Like karma, ch'i is an intangible energy force that greatly affects our lives and how well we live. If you maximize your ch'i, you can reduce negative energy and increase your luck. And this will not only help you in your readings, it will also help you live life happily and to the fullest.

Yin and Yang

▲ Yin and yang.

You've seen the symbol—a circle half white, half black. The black half is yin: negative energy, night, dark, cold, and quiet. The white half, yang, is just the opposite: positive energy, day, light, sunny, hot, and lively.

Together, yin and yang represent balance. The ancient Chinese scholars believed that everything in life has both yin and yang energy. The object of feng shui is to make a delicate equilibrium of the two. You don't want too much of one or the other. (In the home, it is always better to have a bit extra yang than yin.)

Feng Shui Tips Made Simple

Feng shui can get very complicated when you start having to figure out directions and your personal elements: north, south, metal, wood. For simplicity's sake, let's concentrate on the things you can work on right away. The following simple tips will help you to balance the yin and yang and to maximize your ch'i.

In the Bedroom

The farther away the bedroom from the front door, the better your stability will be. In the bedroom, the most important place is your bed. Make sure it is not just a mattress and that it has a base. You should never have anything directly above your bed (ceiling fans, shelves, or other furniture) because it would disturb your ch'i. When you place your bed, make sure that if you sit on it, you would see who's entering the room. Furthermore, if there are windows in the room, they should be to the right or the left of the bed, not to the front or at the back. And once you've set up the bed, place money or precious stones underneath for good luck.

In the Kitchen

The kitchen is important because it is directly linked with the luck, fortune, and prosperity of those living in the home. If you are buying a new house, make sure that the kitchen is not in the basement. The best placement would be on the main floor, in the back section of the house. In the kitchen, the stove should never face the main door, a toilet, or a water pipe. And make sure you don't have any mirrors in your kitchen.

Dining Room

The best placement of the dining room is in the center of your home. It should never be too near the front door. One large mirror in the dining room should reflect the dining room table and all those who may be seated there. The dining room table should not be placed between two doors, a setup that may lead to discord. Aquariums with live fish bring wealth and prosperity into a home. If you do have an aquarium, make sure it does not face the front door.

FACT

There are many Chinese businessmen who, even today, use the art of feng shui to help increase their wealth, luck, and prosperity. Many of them won't sign a contract without first maximizing their good ch'i energy. The presence of fish tanks in many Chinese businesses is an example of feng shui in current practice.

The Guidance of Angels

Have you ever had the feeling of being guided by a force outside yourself? Have you ever sensed that there was something magical around you, gently lifting your energy and spirit? Angels have existed since the creation of the universe. Throughout time, people of different religions and cultures have sought truths about these mystical beings. Though they all had different ideas about them, no religion or culture has ever doubted the existence of angels.

The word "angel" comes from the Greek *angelos,* which means "messenger." Angels are messengers of goodness. They offer guidance, protection, and help. They are beings of light, said to be closest to the universal spirit.

Angels only come when they are most needed, but angelic energy is around you at all times. It offers you assistance if you are willing to listen. This energy connects to you through the advice, touch, or gesture of a friend, a family member, or a stranger; a pet; a dream; or even through yourself. It's more than a gut instinct—it's a message of some idea or concept that comes to you in an instant. It tells you what you should do next or where you should go. Angelic energy can be tapped into if you have the desire and the willingness to connect to it, and it can aid you immensely in divination and in your life.

What Do Angels Look Like?

Italian Renaissance geniuses Botticelli and Leonardo da Vinci would have us believe that angels are the beautiful creatures depicted in their works of art—humanlike beings with white flowing gowns and feathery wings. Maybe they are. Maybe that's what they look like. Certainly, these angels came from a mystical place: the artist's imagination.

But we don't really know whether or not angels really look like that, and that isn't of much significance. The important truth is that we have a symbol to recognize this divine creature. The image with the sweet face, slight smile, flowers in the hair, and wings has become a universal symbol, which we can use to contact angels.

Angelic Power

Not everyone has an angel. Angels normally come to us when we are incredibly vulnerable, perhaps because it's the one time we're sincerely open. But all of us are protected by angelic energy. What's the difference? Angels can help you without being by your side. This is the power of the angels: angelic energy. We can receive strength, guidance, and advice from the angels even when they're far away.

Because a symbol is as powerful as you make it, you can use statues and figures to manifest the energy of the real angels. Just having angel forms near you will bring joy and protection into your life. You don't need to touch them. It's best to have the angel on a high ledge, where it can watch over you.

And since the statue of the angel is so important, you need to choose one that really speaks to you. When you're buying one, make sure you wait until you find one that feels right. You can even make them yourself. In fact, it's a good way to have a deeper connection with them.

If you have four angels, place one in each of the four corners of your room, facing toward you. If you like, you can give your angels names. The important thing is that you have the statues, which will attract the help of the real angels.

ALERT!

Always have an angel statue looking on when you're divining. It will help your instinct and energy flow. You'll get a better sense of what's real and what's not.

Contacting Angels

Angels speak to us through divining tools like the Tarot, runes, and I Ching, but keep in mind that they are spirit guides, and are not all-knowing. Listen to the messages you receive and apply the ones you believe to be correct. Angels aren't perfect. They make mistakes, too.

As messengers, angels don't normally show themselves. But they're there. When you're relaxed and calm, you'll hear them speaking to you. Mostly, they'll disguise themselves as suggestions you regard as your own. They like to remind you that you have the power to help yourself. Sometimes we resist—life seems too hard for us to handle. We want to give up. We want their help. But they only want to see us stronger.

Angels know we want to rely on them, but they want the decisions to be our own. They believe our lives mean more to us when we get the sense that we're changing them by ourselves. So when they help, they mostly do it through us. We receive hints and thoughts in a flash. If you trust in yourself and listen to good instinct, you'll soon recognize when the angels are near you, helping you.

Before you go to sleep at night, speak with your angels and ask them for protection. Close your eyes and imagine a light circling around your home. Say: "Angels north and south and east and west. Keep me safe and bring peace this night."

Symbols and Talismans

As you set up your divination area, it helps to have objects that carry special symbolism for you. Talismans are symbolic objects that contain power that you confer upon them. How does that work? Well, take the example of the bogeyman. The bogeyman is created by the child's imagination. Even though no bogeyman has ever had any special powers, every child has experienced the terror of her own private bogeyman—a made-up creature that never quite looks the same to any child around the world. Sometimes children even come up with resourceful ways to rid themselves of this demon—by keeping a night-light on, barring the closet door, doing a quick check under the bed, and so on. By believing in the bogeyman, the children make the creature real and give it power over them.

Channeling Energy Through Symbols

If you give something power, it becomes the symbol you want it to represent. If there is a particular symbol that gives you comfort or makes you feel stronger, keep it near to you. Though certain symbols have universal meaning, only those that feed your positive energy and sharpen your instincts will make a difference. Positive energy needs channeling points. This is what your symbols are used for.

Successful divination requires that you harmonize with the energy around you, and a talisman can help you do that because it concentrates the vibrations of the energy you are trying to focus on. In turn, you wind up on the same frequency level as the positive energy you've assigned to your symbol. Then this good energy is channeled through you and into the cards or runes.

Choosing Your Symbol

Lions are very powerful protectors. For hundreds of years, it has not been uncommon for homes to have lion or lioness statues on both sides of the entranceway. Though lions are esthetically pleasing, they were not put there for this reason. Lions are fierce, proud animals. People believed they were protectors. They could ward off bad luck and watch over them. If lions are a symbol that you relate to, place a small statue in your bedroom. A stuffed animal will do the job just as well if that's more your style. You may find that having any sort of lion figure in your room ups your courage in general. And if your sun sign happens to be Leo, you'll benefit even more from this powerful symbol.

FACT

In many ancient cultures, diviners relied on drums, feathers, fire, and other sacred objects as their talismans—to channel their energy and make their predictions. You don't have to use the same tools, as long as you find the talismans that are right for you.

Many cultures and religions have their own symbols. In Taoism, a statue of a horse in the dining room is said to bring good luck (and good feng shui); an elephant with its trunk facing up is also said to have strong effects on luck and fortune. Whether it's a talisman you wear on your body, a stuffed animal that means something significant to you, or a bust of Wolfgang Amadeus Mozart, a symbol in your house is worth the time it takes to find one: Your instinct, your well-being, and your readings will benefit immensely from it.

Chapter 6

The Tarot

When you think of divination, what's the first thing that comes to mind? For many people, the answer is the Tarot. A deck of Tarot cards can provide you with a symbolic way to tap into the unknown by focusing on the mystical energy that surrounds the cards and the card spreads. When it comes to Tarot, your subconscious is your guide. In this chapter, discover how Tarot cards work and how to use them in divining the future.

History and Allure

The Tarot first appeared in Italy in the fourteenth century as a card game called *tarocco*. As the game gained popularity, well-to-do patrons (and believers) commissioned artists to design beautiful decks on their behalf. One such famous deck is that of the Visconti-Sforza, created in the mid-1400s.

Soon, psychics began to use the Tarot for divination, and this method of fortunetelling remained popular up to the 1800s, when European nobility would make appointments on the other side of town, flocking to dilapidated huts where old crones dressed in rags resided. These "witches"—surrounded by toads, owls, and black cats—would set down the cards and tell them their fortunes.

Then, in the early 1900s, the Tarot was adopted by many secret societies, including the Hermetic Order of the Golden Dawn. One of the leading members of this magical order, Arthur Edward Waite, created a Tarot deck that remains popular to this day—the Rider-Waite deck.

Gateway to the Unknown

Aside from the powerful, beautiful images the cards depict, they also serve to stir the imagination, tap into the subconscious, and heighten the intuitive state. They can be used for meditation as well as for divination because they work as a gateway—important messages are conveyed through the symbols of universal life, from birth to death and all the everyday experiences in the middle.

A great deal of mystery surrounds the symbolism of the Tarot, but one thing is certain: Their power is as strong as the ability of the person using them (as long as it's done correctly). Done right, the Tarot can warn you, give you advice, and tell you of the possibilities of your future.

The Cards and What They Mean

The traditional Tarot deck has seventy-eight cards. There are twenty-two Major Arcana or Trump cards, numbered from zero to twenty-one (XXI). Each card corresponds to an archetype of human life, and the cards have names like The Moon and The Devil. In addition, the Tarot deck contains fifty-six Minor Arcana cards, which are divided into four suits of Cups, Wands, Swords, and Pentacles. In turn, each suit has fourteen cards, from Ace through X and Page, Knight, Queen, and King.

The images on the cards may, at first, seem obscure or esoteric, but they are there to represent common universal truths. They speak of the same cycles and experiences we have encountered since the beginning of time—experiences that have been depicted by early civilizations in ancient drawings, paintings, and sculpture. The imagery in the cards ranges from birth and foolishness to growing, changing, gaining wisdom, and even death; and each card tells its own story. But it's through the combination of the cards that we divine and make our interpretations.

ALERT!

Although each card has its own meaning and its own interpretation, you need to trust your own instinct. Study the cards and their original interpretation. Then, if a certain card strikes you in a particular fashion and you intuit a different meaning for it, go with your intuition. Your inner voice is probably correct.

In general, when you read the Tarot cards, it's important to keep in mind that the Major Arcana cards are a bit more important than those of the Minor Arcana—or, to be more precise, the Major Arcana are more fixed. Minor Arcana cards represent events that you have control over and can change. Major Arcana cards, on the other hand, are said to be fated, and generally represent what will happen no matter what you try to do to avoid it.

Reversed Readings

There are two ways you can read the cards: with or without interpreting them differently when they're reversed. When a card appears upside down, some readers simply turn it around, but others believe that reversed cards have a different meaning. In the beginning, it's usually better to lay all the cards with the right side up, without getting into how the reversed cards change the interpretation and meaning, but do whatever feels more comfortable. Many times the reversed cards are simply the negative aspect of the card's original meaning. Decide what's best for you.

The Major Arcana

The Fool (0)

The fool is a youthful soul, with bright, multicolored garb (like that of a court jester), and his card indicates that it's time to take a risk and go with the flow; it's about adventure and putting it all out on the line. If the outcome cards surrounding it are negative, The Fool could mean the opposite: a warning against taking this risk. Ask a more specific question to get a clear response about it. This card also refers to spontaneity and taking a chance in love or any new experience. Normally, it speaks about adventure, fun, and risk without consequences.

The Magician (I)

This is a card of new beginnings, opportunities, and good communication. If your question is "Will he call?" or "Should I contact this person?" The Magician in the Future column with favorable outcome cards means yes.

When The Magician appears in a reading, it also signifies that you need to evaluate your options and balance different areas of your life better. For example, your love life and your career should be tied in together in a more equal fashion.

The High Priestess (II)

This is a card of secret agendas and hidden meaning. It is associated with the moon and, therefore, also hints at mystery and secrets. If you see this card, the Tarot is telling you to trust your hunches and intuition. The High Priestess card may also refer to an ideal mate.

The Empress (III)

This card indicates motherhood, fertility, or anything of a nurturing nature, and can warn of or predict pregnancy. If the querent is a man, this card indicates that there is a woman in his life whom he sees as a type of mother figure, either for himself or for others. The Empress can also signify a solid, happy relationship.

The Emperor (IV)

This card is the masculine counterpart to The Empress. It signifies authoritative power, dominance, and confidence. It tells of maintaining control and using your influence in order to help steer things in the right direction.

FACT

In 1910, Arthur Edward Waite, creator of the Rider-Waite Tarot cards, wrote, "The Tarot embodies symbolical presentations of universal ideas, behind which lie all the implicits of the human mind."

The Hierophant (V)

The Hierophant, also known as The High Priest or Pope card, is the male counterpart to II, The High Priestess card. You should take as advice any cards following this card. The Hierophant also indicates that you'll have success if you follow the rules.

The Lovers (VI)

Normally, this card represents the spiritual love union of two people, but it could also signal emotional choices you need to make or a physical attraction and a purely physical union between two people.

The Chariot (VII)

The Chariot is a card that represents action. If you're asking questions about whether or not you'll move soon or if there is travel in your future and this card comes up, the answer is yes. The Chariot also stands for progress and success against the odds.

Justice (VIII)

The Justice card tells you that a decision needs to be made by weighing your options and that balance is the key. If you have any pending legal matters, getting this card in a reading is a sign that they will be resolved, and whatever the question, the result will be fair (in a karmic sense) even if not favorable.

The Hermit (IX)

This is a card of peace, tranquility, and going it alone. If your question is "Should I act now?" the answer is "No. Wait. You need to do things on your own first." The Hermit also signifies looking inside yourself to find answers.

The Wheel of Fortune (X)

Luck is on your side. What you want can be yours. Fate will play a big part in the way things will work out. Changes are coming soon, and things will take a turn for the better.

Strength (XI)

This card signifies quiet confidence, good health, and taking pride in yourself and your actions. It could also mean strong physical attraction to a love interest (on either or both sides). Be patient and continue with the path you're on. This is a positive card.

Many Major Arcana turning up in one reading signify that the timing really isn't up to you (or the querent). Because these Trump cards have a lot to do with destiny, it means that there are outside influences determining when they will happen. Trust that they will happen when the timing is right.

The Hanged Man (XII)

This card sometimes points to ego getting in the way of things. If you're asking advice on what to do about a potential partner and this card comes out, it means you might have to stroke his or her ego to get ahead with this person. This is also a "wait" card if you're asking whether or not to take action. Everything has stopped due to complications. You need to change something and make good decisions in order for the tides to turn.

Death (XIII)

This card is not as threatening as you might think it is—it signifies change, the end of one period and the break before the next one. When you pull this card in a reading, it sometimes means that the querent must give up something in order to move ahead.

Temperance (XIV)

This card signifies patience and balance. Go slowly and weigh your options. Things will be okay, but the timing of it is not up to you.

The Devil (XV)

More than anything, The Devil is a karma card. If you ask if it was the destiny of "this-and-this" to happen and this card comes out, the answer is yes. In marriage, this is a good card because it also signifies a situation that you're bound to. Other interpretations can be negative, depending on the other cards: greed, bad intentions, lust, or anger.

The Tower (XVI)

This is another change card. It warns that things may have to hit rock bottom before you can learn from what happened and start over again. This can be a small change or a drastic, serious change. Sometimes it signifies the end of a relationship or getting fired from a particular job. It also means that there are outside influences affecting the situation over which you have no control.

The Star (XVII)

The Star is a wish card and a good omen. It is saying that you should know what you want and go for it. The outcome should be favorable, depending on the other cards. The Star also means that you'll be good at getting around the obstacles that are seemingly in your way in a particular situation.

The Moon (XVIII)

This card deals with emotions and may signal that your emotions are getting in the way or helping you with the situation. The Moon could also stand for obsession, self-deceit, or confusion. On rare occasions, it signifies illness, or lack of energy.

The Sun (XIX)

This card always has a positive meaning. In fact, it brightens up the negative cards around it and softens their impact on the situation. The Sun represents success, good luck, happiness, and childlike pleasure.

Judgment (XX)

When this card comes up, you need to re-evaluate what's important to you in the situation. Are your priorities in the right order? The Judgment is a positive card because it means that, in the end, your choice will probably be the right one. There are other factors at work here, helping you. This card also affects those around it, because it speeds up their timing.

The World (XXI)

This is one of the most positive cards of the Major Arcana. It signifies spiritual enlightenment. It completes the life journey in the Tarot, which starts from birth (The Fool, or 0). This card represents success and reward. Things will go smoothly from here on in.

Before you do a reading, have the querent pick a Court card (Page, Knight, Queen, or King) to refer to herself. For example, a woman with a fire sun sign may pick the Queen of Wands.

The Minor Arcana

The Minor Arcana include Cups, Wands, Swords, and Pentacles. Each suit represents an element: Wands refers to fire, cups to water, pentacles to earth, and swords to air. Here are descriptions for each of the cards, organized by suit.

Cups

Ace: The beginning of a romance or love. Things are going well.

II (love): A good partnership.

III (friendship): Fun, or a reunion with someone from your past.

IV (boredom): Also represents emotional withdrawal.

V (sorrow): Taking time out alone so that you can heal emotionally.

VI (nostalgic feelings): The past has influence over your present situation.

VII (superficiality): Things may not be as they seem, or you have too many choices.

VIII (leaving behind): Letting go of something so that you may continue on your spiritual journey.

IX (the wish card): Indication of success and happiness—that you'll get what you want.

X (the ultimate): Marriage, real love, contentment, tranquility, and completion.

Page: A new courtship or friendship will arrive soon.

Knight: An invitation or a new partner. It normally refers to a young, brown-haired man with light eyes.

Queen: A woman who is intuitive and sensual. She is a sweet dark-haired woman with light eyes.

King: A man who gives good advice and is creative. A kindly brown-haired older man with light eyes.

QUESTION?

What if the outcome doesn't seem to answer the question?
If you're getting all pentacle cards when you're asking questions about love (cups), there are three possible explanations: Work or money is affecting the problem; you're asking one question and thinking of another; or the cards are trying to tell you something. Ask another question.

Wands

Ace: Good beginnings for work or a new idea. Fresh energy.

II (waiting): Things can go well but prepare yourself for obstacles.

III (success): Specifically, this card represents success in a group venture. Be confident and know what you want.

IV (change of residence): May refer to a move related to marriage and so can represent celebration and pleasure.

V (difficulties): You can overcome these if you change your strategy.

VI (public recognition): Gratification and awards for a job well done.

VII (resourcefulness): You need to be resourceful and competitive to reach your goal.

VIII (speed): Represents movement and signals that things are going along smoothly. This card speeds up everything in the reading.

IX (standing your ground): Keep your principles and discipline firm.

X (burdens): You've taken on too much responsibility.

Page: A younger person who wants to help you with work and business.

Knight: A person who has a message for you; someone you can trust.

Queen: A fair-haired woman who can help you in business. She's friendly, loyal, and mature.

King: An influential light-haired man who is willing to help you. He brings good news and luck.

There are a few general points that you can keep in mind when you decipher Minor Arcana cards. Aces always stand for good new beginnings. Tens represent completion of a cycle. Knights are messengers and refer to news you'll receive soon. Cups normally refer to love, wands to emotional journeys, swords to overcoming problems and strife, and pentacles to work, money, and stability.

Swords

Ace: The start of victory. Keep going and you'll be successful.

II (peace): Communication will help the situation. You need to face the truth.

III (heartbreak): A love affair that is ending. It's time to let go and move on.

IV (a time out): Take a break from the situation—you need to recover from emotional pain.

V (honesty): Be courageous but honest. Deception is not the way to win.

VI (a positive move): Leaving your emotional rocky past behind for the better.

VII (betrayal and mistrust): This card warns you to be wary of shady dealings.

VIII (fear): Your insecurities are keeping you or your mate behind.

IX (depression and loneliness): Sometimes indicates bad dreams.

X (end): It could mean failure or the end of a cycle. There is nothing positive left in the situation.

Page: Someone who brings you problems or is spying on you.

Knight: An argument is on the horizon. This card usually refers to a dark-haired young man with light eyes.

Queen: A woman you can't trust. Many times, she is dark-haired with light eyes.

King: A man of power who is dark-haired with light eyes. He speaks well and offers answers through communication.

ALERT!

People or Court cards (Page, Knight, Queen, and King) don't necessarily refer to a person. They can also refer to a way you or another person is dealing with a situation. You should interpret the meaning based on the cards surrounding the Court card.

Pentacles

Ace: An excellent start in business, or stability. Finances are looking up.

II (smooth changes): Everything will go smoothly. A good business indication, but it can also refer to other areas.

III (the works): Approval from a work colleague or boss. Hang in there.

IV (harnessing your power): You need to move forward for success. Don't be inflexible. It also signifies home stability or a possible move.

V (anxiety): Loss of money or self-respect. This could also be a warning.

VI (success): Giving or getting good advice or help where it is needed. It can refer to any area, including financial.

VII (failure): Money problems; bad omens in general. Your efforts are fruitless. You need to take another tack.

VIII (prudence): You're incorporating your old beliefs with the new ones. This is also a warning to tread slowly and not waste too much energy and/or money on the problem.

IX (earning power): Tranquility, financial security, and a period of enjoying your hard work and accomplishments. A break from worry.

X (perfect richness): Complete home, financial, and work stability. Good money relations or possible inheritance.

Page: Good news about money or a job. A dark-haired young man with dark eyes.

Knight: A young dark-haired man at work may have a message for you.

Queen: A practical woman who is generous and fair. Normally, she has dark hair and dark eyes.

King: An honest man with financial security. He can give good advice and has dark hair and dark eyes.

FACT

Pentacles refer to money, finances, work, and stability. They also refer to material and spiritual possessions. The Pentacle Court cards can refer to someone with dark features or to someone with an earth sign—Capricorn, Taurus, or Virgo.

Shuffling the Tarot

Is there one right way to shuffle the Tarot cards? Not really. The most important thing to understand about shuffling the cards is that they need to be shuffled well. In other words, your energy, the question, and the situation you're reflecting on all need to be "felt" by the cards. There's no other way to describe it. While you shuffle, the cards actually absorb your emotions, energy, and mood. Stop shuffling only when you feel that the time is right. Whether it takes thirty seconds or ten minutes until you're ready, that's how long you need to shuffle. Only then will you get a clear reading.

Here are some additional tips for shuffling the cards:

- **Relax.** If you're stressed or anxious, your feelings will affect the cards.
- **Have a clear question in mind.** If you're asking one question but thinking of another, the cards will reflect your indecision.
- **Keep your emotions in check.** Cards pick up emotions all too easily. Clear your head and try not to think too much about how you feel.
- **Focus.** Say the question out loud if doing so helps you to focus.
- **Have a spread in mind before you lay out the cards.** Choosing a spread that's right for the kind of question you're asking will give you a clearer answer.

Whether or not you want the person you're reading for to shuffle the cards is up to you. You can do it, as long as you're both concentrating on the question at hand. If they insist, keep an extra deck around that you can use for when you do readings for others.

Before you start, you must decide which way you're going to pick the cards. You can either deal them off the top or spread them out like a fan. Normally, if the querent shuffles the cards, you take them off the top. If you shuffle, have the person choose from the fanned-out cards.

The Spreads

There are many spreads out there, and they're all based on one thing: personal interpretation. The Celtic Cross spread is the most traditional, but it's possible to find twenty different variations on how it's laid out. The solution? You can use the ones described in this book or create some of your own. The key is to decide beforehand on all of the meanings and to be consistent.

In each spread, Card 1 is known as the Significator. Your entire reading focuses around this card, because it describes the crux of the situation, what the problem is based on. If the Significator is The Eight of Swords (the fear card), it is probable that the querent is not moving ahead with the situation because of insecurities holding him back.

The Celtic Cross Spread

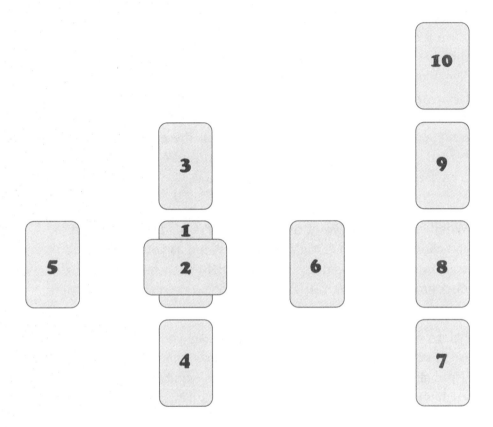

▲ The Celtic Cross spread.

Card 1:   The heart of the matter.
Card 2:   The problems or possibilities you have concerning the situation.
Card 3:   Advice related to the question.
Card 4:   Influences that have affected you in the past.
Card 5:   Things that are affecting you now.
Card 6:   The current state of the situation.
Card 7:   How other people near you regard the situation.
Card 8:   What will happen regarding the question in the next three months.
Card 9:   What you might go through in order to get what you want.
Card 10:   The future outcome.

The Spread of Past, Present, and Future

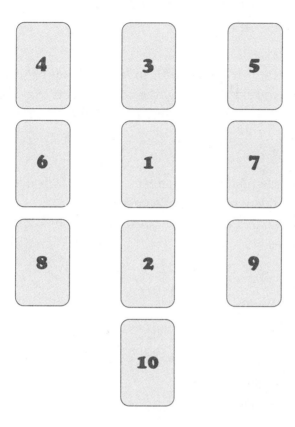

▲ The spread of past, present, and future.

The general past, present, and future overview spread is handy because you're looking at the big picture, not the meaning of each card, which helps you to intuit better. With this spread, it's the combination of the cards that carries the meaning.

In the spread, Card 1 is your Significator, and refers to the heart of the question. Cards 4, 6, and 8 are in your "past" column, with Card 8 representing the most recent past (it could be referring to what happened yesterday in regard to the question). Cards 3, 1, 2, and 10 are the "present" cards, but they also refer to recent past and short-term future. They signify the happenings going on in the period right now, regarding the question. Cards 5, 7, and 9 refer to what is going to happen in the future.

Cards 9 and 10 should be the main cards to watch. These are your final outcome cards. Card 10 is referring to present outcome and Card 9 is your final outcome card.

ALERT!

It doesn't matter if the querent is in front of you or sitting to one side. You should always lay the cards out so that they're facing you. This way, it will be less awkward for you when you're reading them.

Let's try a sample reading. Alexander has come to you to ask, "What will happen in my relationship with Beatrice?"

You lay out the cards in the past, present, and future spread, and you get the following results:

Card 1:   Death
Card 2:   Five of Wands
Card 3:   Six of Cups
Card 4:   Seven of Pentacles
Card 5:   Ace of Cups
Card 6:   Knight of Swords
Card 7:   Eight of Wands
Card 8:   The Fool
Card 9:   The World
Card 10:   The Hanged Man

First, you take a look at the cards that represent the past, in the left column of the spread (4, 6, and 8):

- The Seven of Pentacles indicates that Alexander had problems, either with Beatrice or in a different relationship.
- The Knight of Swords is a person who got in the way in the past—an ex-boyfriend, a coworker, or a family member.

- The Fool signals that Alexander made a "leap of the heart" in the past in his relationship with Beatrice, because he was burned either by her or by another woman.

Next, take a look at the present (Cards 3, 1, 2, and 10). They show the current state of affairs:

- The Six of Cups indicates that there is pleasure involved in this relationship.
- Death indicates that the situation is in a process of change right now.
- The Five of Wands warns that they might have had or will soon have problems, a fight, or a minor discussion concerning their relationship.
- The Hanged Man refers to a waiting period in order for things to move forward. It could also indicate that his or her ego is getting in the way.

Now, go on to the future outcome column (Cards 5, 7, and 9):

- The Ace of Cups means the relationship will have good beginnings toward love. Either the relationship has changed for the better or it is on the verge of getting more serious.
- The Eight of Wands means that once it starts, it will happen quickly.
- The World as an outcome card is the best you can get. It means everything will be wonderful.

Keep in mind that the Major Arcana are the fixed cards and represent destiny, while the Minor Arcana are things that are changeable. In the past, present, and future spread, the Major Arcana cards that turned up were Death, The Hanged Man, and The World. Therefore, the main response to this question is based on the position of these three cards.

Quick Three-Card Spread

▲ Quick three-card spread.

In this simple spread, the first card refers to your past, the second card to your present, and the third to your future. Look at the "future" (outcome) card first. If it's positive, take the "present" card as advice.

For instance, let's say your friend Julie wants to know if she should call John. You shuffle your Tarot, and lay out a quick three-card spread with the following cards:

Card 1:   Ten of Cups
Card 2:   Two of Pentacles
Card 3:   The Sun

The "past" card, Ten of Cups, signals that things were good in the past between the two of them (or that Julie has a positive, healthy attitude about the past). The "present" card, Two of Pentacles, shows that there seem to be no problems and that there is no need to worry. The "future" card, The Sun, is a great outcome card. Nothing Julie can do will hurt her or the relationship regarding the question. Your response: Yes, you can call him if you want. Either way, things will work out fine.

ALERT!

Relating the cards to the question can be tricky. In the three-card spread example, the cards say that the outcome will be good for Julie, but this could mean any number of things. If, for instance, they had broken up, making the phone call could mean getting back together, or that Julie would learn something from the phone call that would make it easier for her to get over John.

Tarot Timing

The truth is that it's very difficult to determine the timing of events with Tarot cards, but it's important to pay attention to the windows of opportunity. Always remember that free will affects destiny. If you're supposed to take action and you don't, you could miss the chance you were meant to have.

Also keep in mind that things don't happen until you're spiritually ready for them. If your question is "When will I meet The One?" and there are many Major Arcana cards indicating that you will meet The One soon, be prepared. If you haven't resolved other issues of your life, it may push back the timing of this meeting. It will still happen, but it will happen later.

One woman had a reading done and the psychic told her that her boyfriend would propose in the next two months. It didn't happen. Instead, they broke up. She had some intimacy issues that she needed to confront. Two years later, they met up again by chance, got back together, and he proposed. It can happen. You have to be ready in order for the good things in your life to come about.

Time Indicators

Normally, Tarot card readings are indicating things that will happen within the next three months. But there are other indicators you can look for. Look at the last card you put down. If it's a Major Arcana card or a Court card, go backwards through the other cards you laid out until you come to a Minor Arcana card.

Then, look at that Minor Arcana card. An Ace refers to one, a Two to two, and so forth. Is it Wands, Cups, Pentacles, or Swords? Wands refer to weeks, Cups to days, Pentacles to years, and Swords to months. So, for example, Two of Wands means two weeks, and Five of Cups means five days. (E)

Chapter 7

See the Future Inside a Crystal

Crystals are very powerful. Simply put, they're the gems of the earth. You can use them for meditation, to increase energy and intuition, for healing, and, of course, for divination. In this chapter, learn everything from how crystals work for spiritual healing to their role in scrying, or seeing into the future.

Look into My Crystal Ball

A crystal ball is a clear, nearly transparent piece of quartz used to stimulate the subconscious mind and to put the reader into a kind of semihypnotic state. Although anyone can practice divination with a crystal ball, most often the users are those who already possess psychic intuition.

Crystal balls were used long before the age of modern psychics or even those street fortunetellers. In India and China, crystal gazers were revered members of their community. They lived a monastic life, refraining from sexual indulgences, certain foods, alcohol, and other "evil" devices that people believed could decrease the crystal gazer's divining powers. Scrying arrived in Europe around the fifth century, and forms of scrying were also practiced by the Mayans and the North American Indians.

FACT

Another name for crystal ball gazing is "crystallomancy." Diviners from ancient Babylon, India, and Greece also used other objects for scrying—still pools of water, red wine, shiny surfaces, glass, ink, black mirrors, fire, wet slate, and bowls of water.

Get Ready for a Reading

If you're ready to invest in a crystal ball, make sure to check around first and get an idea of what a competitive price may be. Buying a smaller one will reduce the cost. Though the larger ones may help you reach a more relaxed, intuitive state, a smaller one will do this almost as well.

Once you've got your crystal ball, here is what you need to do in order to get ready for crystal ball gazing:

- Sit up straight in a chair, feet planted firmly on the ground.
- Make sure that the room is at a comfortable temperature.
- The lights should be low, with absolutely no direct sunlight entering the room.
- There should be no glittering, distracting objects in the room. The room must be an open space without clutter or mess.
- The best time of the day to do this is just before the sun sets.

- There should be no more than three people, including yourself, in the room at one time.
- You can have the crystal on the table or you can hold it in your hand.

Are you calm, focused, and relaxed? If you're feeling anxious, put off doing the reading for another time. The key is to say what first comes to mind and find the meaning in it afterwards. On some occasions, you may not get an answer right away. Other times, the vision will be shockingly clear. In the beginning, you should do shorter sittings, since crystal ball gazing requires a lot of energy. Gradually, you'll be able to sit longer.

Let the Divination Begin

Here are the steps to successful crystal ball reading:

1. Close your eyes for one or two minutes (or longer, if needed) to help clear your head of all thoughts.
2. Open your eyes and blink normally.
3. You can pass your left hand and then your right hand over the crystal to stimulate the circulating energy.
4. Look calmly into the crystal. The backdrop should fade away before you start seeing visions.
5. Have the querent ask a direct question.
6. Say what you see. If the vision is not clear or is broken, stop.

Interpretations

There are many possible images you can see in the crystal. In order to interpret them, consult Chapter 13 (on dreams) and Chapter 14 (on tealeaf readings), since symbol meaning is universal. Trust your instinct as well as your common sense. If you see a heart with a dagger through it, for example, it indicates love, heartbreak, and suffering. Visions seen toward the right of the crystal ball are symbolic, whereas ones to the left are meant to indicate real-life situations. Visions near the front indicate the near future; visions near the back indicate the past.

Here are some other tips to keep in mind:

- Clouds of white or blue are good omens.
- Rising visions hint at improvement of things to come.
- Seeing the sun predicts success or good fortune.
- A snake foretells that someone close to the querent is deceitful.
- Yellow clouds indicate jealousy.
- Red clouds warn the querent of impending danger.
- Green clouds indicate hope and good finances.

FACT

Carl Gustav Jung stated, "Your visions will become clear only when you can look into your own heart. [He] who looks outside, dreams; [he] who looks inside, awakens."

Special Crystals

In addition to using a crystal ball, many fortunetellers rely on a set of crystals. As you collect crystals for the purposes of healing and divination, make sure that each crystal has a special significance for you. If not, you're only buying overpriced rocks. Pick crystals you feel drawn to—after a little time, the reason for the attraction will be revealed. You can carry the crystals around with you in a little pouch, in your pocket, or around your neck.

Crystals come in many varieties, and each has a special meaning and appropriate uses:

- **Agate:** A form of quartz, it prevents headaches and brings good health and luck.
- **Amber:** Fossilized tree resin, which gives protection, strength, courage, and stability to whoever wears it.
- **Amethyst:** This violet quartz has a soothing, calming effect and is said to change slightly in color depending on who wears it.
- **Aquamarine:** A light blue stone, it is meant to bring luck to sea voyagers and to bring peace to your love life.

- **Bloodstone:** A red-dotted stone used to encourage blood clotting on wounds in ancient times. It helps in protection, to encourage good finance and career moves, and to aid processes in the body when worn close.
- **Coral:** A pink or red stone from the Mediterranean Sea. Coral is said to help prevent illness and can protect you against ill-wishers.
- **Diamond:** The hardest stone in existence, it signifies purity, strength, and longevity.
- **Emerald:** This green stone was believed to carry powers for attaining good health, easing pain, and protecting against bad intentions.
- **Garnet:** This dark red stone may protect the wearer against ill health. If you receive this crystal as a gift, it may strengthen the friendship between you and the gift-giver.
- **Lapis lazuli:** A blue stone with specks. This crystal may prevent and cure pain and tension headaches.
- **Pearl:** A precious stone found in the shell of certain seawater inhabitants such as mussels or oysters (with one exception: "cultured pearls" are made artificially). Pearls symbolize trust and purity, protect against evil and danger, and help the wearer clarify emotions.
- **Ruby:** This deep red or pink stone provides a positive outlook on life and wards off bad dreams.
- **Sapphire:** A stone that varies in color from white or colorless (rare) to blue. Sapphires give balance and eloquence of speech.
- **Serpentine:** An opaque stone with tints of yellow or green. It is meant for protection against nature (such as bee stings and snake bites), and may reduce swelling.
- **Topaz:** A stone that comes in different colors, it protects against infection and ensures fidelity in marriage. Some also use it to cure insomnia.
- **Turquoise:** This stone, which has lent its name to a color, is used for protection against evil and gives fortitude to the wearer.

Crystals pick up negative and positive energies, so it's wise to cleanse them once in a while. You can perform a cleansing with one of four methods: fire (lighting a black candle near them), earth (burying them in soil for a few days), air (leaving them exposed to the full or new moon), or water (in a riverbed or a stream).

Multicolor Gems

Other, less popular crystals that you can use both for healing and for divination (by casting, which we'll discuss a little later) include the following:

- **Aventurine:** In divination, this crystal signals good luck, a time of peace, or money coming in—a change for the better.
- **Beryl:** Use this crystal to help prevent people from gossiping about you. Some psychics also employ it in love healing.
- **Blue agate:** Use this gem to help you solve childhood issues or problems with children. Blue agate in divination signals a need to communicate or find out the truth.
- **Carnelian**: In divination, this stone warns you of sickness. It may also signal a return of courage and may be taken as advice to find a new mentor.
- **Citrine:** This crystal can help you improve your memory and aid in thought analysis, psychic awareness, and intuition.
- **Chrysoprase:** In divination, this crystal brings you advice to get more involved in a particular hobby or interest you have.
- **Green jasper:** In divination, it brings a warning that fears are holding you back.
- **Malachite:** This gem can help you in business. In divination, it represents success that will result from hard work.
- **Orange agate:** In divination, it tells you that you need to be more social, or that you should expect a reunion with someone from the past.

- **Pink jasper:** In divination, it advises you to seek help from someone older.
- **Purple agate:** In divination, this gem represents vulnerability and reminds you to have faith.
- **Rhodonite:** Brings happy tidings of luck and of good things to come.
- **Rose quartz:** In divination, signals luck in love and relationships; may also represent a surprise from a friend.
- **Tiger's eye:** Represents protection from an unknown source and reminds you to draw on your inner strength; may also relate to matters of education.
- **Yellow quartz:** In divination, this gem carries the meaning of spirituality, happiness, and the end of a negative cycle.

Crystals and the Sun Signs

Particular crystals are especially beneficial to certain people, depending on their sun sign.

Sun Sign	Crystal	Sun Sign	Crystal
Aries	bloodstone, diamond	Libra	lapis lazuli
Taurus	turquoise	Scorpio	aquamarine
Gemini	topaz	Sagittarius	garnet, quartz crystal
Cancer	pearl	Capricorn	ruby
Leo	aquamarine, amber	Aquarius	garnet
Virgo	serpentine	Pisces	amethyst, coral

Easy Casting

To use your crystals to foretell the future, you can rely on a method known as casting. Note that if you use it to read for yourself, you can only do so a few times. Once you know the meanings of each individual crystal, you'll be drawn to particular crystals subconsciously in order to get suitable interpretations. Of course, you can always use the casting circle in doing a reading for newcomers.

ALERT!

Keep your crystals in anything made of a natural or earth substance. Stoneware jars work well. A pouch made of raw material such as cotton or hemp would be appropriate, too. You want your crystals to be in neutral surroundings so that they won't be influenced by other energies.

The Casting Circle

To cast a circle, place your crystals randomly in a large circle. Then put a plain white, orange, or pink candle in the center. Pick the color of the candle according to what kind of question you want to ask. In general, green is for money and finance questions, pink is for love, and white is good for any kind of random question. (For a review of color meanings, refer back to Chapter 5.)

Take a few seconds to relax. Close your eyes and think only of the question you want to ask. Don't imagine the response, just the question itself. Then, open your eyes and light the candle with a match. The first crystal that catches the light (and your eye) is your answer. Look up the meaning to get your interpretation.

Crystal Messages

You've already had an introduction to the meanings behind each gem and crystal. Here are the specifics on interpreting crystals during casting:

- **Agate:** Expect money to come from an unexpected source.
- **Amber:** Keep your feet firmly planted on the ground and be confident in moving ahead with your plans.
- **Amethyst:** Someone close to you may be out to make trouble.
- **Aquamarine:** Stop doubting your feelings and instead simply trust your instincts and go with the flow.
- **Bloodstone:** Lighten up and don't take yourself too seriously.
- **Coral:** Don't take on too many tasks at one time.
- **Diamond:** Represents constancy in love or heralds the arrival of a new partner.

- **Emerald:** Someone will make a promise to you and keep it.
- **Garnet:** Warns that false friendships are getting the best of you.
- **Lapis lazuli:** Determination will help you succeed with your plans in the upcoming future.
- **Pearl:** Serves as a gentle reminder that communication is the only way to solve the problem.
- **Ruby:** A new opportunity in love or career will soon present itself.
- **Sapphire:** Beware of fraud and/or false words.
- **Serpentine:** Unless you change your path, problems you are currently having will happen again.
- **Topaz:** Trust your hunches—they are correct.
- **Turquoise:** Don't worry so much, things will turn out well.

You can also use divining crystals the same way you cast runes (see Chapter 9). The Tarot card spreads, in Chapter 6, are good to use with crystals, too. Try the past, present, and future three-card (or three-crystal) spread. Then, consult the meanings for the crystals found in this chapter and make your interpretations.

The Seven Chakras

According to the Hindu tradition, a *chakra* is an energy field, and each human being is affected by its flows of negative and positive vibrations. Each person has seven main chakras, each located in a different part of the body. If your chakras are all working correctly, you feel good and your energy is up. When you feel tired, overly emotional, creatively blocked, or angry without reason, one of your chakras may be lacking in positive energy. Such a state is not conducive to divination and is bad in terms of your general well-being.

What does this have to do with crystals? Well, crystals have healing powers that help you to balance your chakras. By holding the crystal for ten to twenty-five minutes over a region of the body that corresponds with the chakra in need, you can correct the bad energy and fix the problem.

The functioning and interaction of your chakras create what is known as your aura, the electromagnetic field that surrounds your body. The aura produces a slightly colored haze or light around the person. Though some people can see it, most people cannot. Talented psychics can sometimes diagnose what may be wrong in a person's life based on her aura.

If you want to try to read someone's aura, have them stand in a sunlit room against a stark white background. Stare at a point just above or to the side of the person until you lose focus and your eyes blur somewhat. Is there a haze of light around them? What color is it? What you are seeing is the person's aura.

The First Chakra

Also known as the "base" or "root" chakra, the first chakra is located at the base of the spine, at the coccyx bone. When it is working well, it grounds you, gives you strength, and helps you feel connected with the rest of the world. If the first chakra is imbalanced, it can manifest itself with problems such as lower back pain, leg problems, or fear. The aura of this chakra is red. Red crystals of any kind (ruby, garnet, lodestone, flame agate, or red jasper) held over the area for up to half an hour will help stimulate the nerves to balance this chakra.

The Second Chakra

Also known as the "sex" or "sacrum" chakra, it is located at the sex organs, just below the pelvis. When this chakra is in good form, your creativity, sensuality, and intuitions are in top shape. Imbalance of this aura can lead to depression, a self-critical nature, and lack of energy and/or libido. The aura of this chakra is orange. Orange crystals such as coral, rose quartz, fire agate, citrine, and carnelian can help you balance the second chakra.

The Third Chakra

Also known as the "solar plexus" or "stomach" chakra, it is found between the breastbone and the navel. When this chakra is functioning correctly, you can trust your gut feelings, you're calm and confident, and you basically feel good in your own skin. When the third chakra is out of balance, you can feel overly aggressive, have digestion problems, and may doubt your self-control. The aura of this chakra is yellow. Yellow crystals like amber, heliodor, laguna agate, yellow topaz, and jasper will help align this chakra.

The Fourth Chakra

Also known as the "heart" chakra, it is located in the region of the heart. When the fourth chakra is balanced, your energy is great and you feel happy with yourself and with others. When the fourth chakra is off keel, you can feel anxiety, on edge, or have pains in your chest. The aura of this chakra is green. Green crystals such as emerald, jade, malachite, tourmaline, and aventurine will do wonders for this chakra.

The Fifth Chakra

Also known as the "throat" chakra, this energy field is located in the general region of your throat. When this chakra is on the mark, your mental processes are working well and you're able to express your thoughts eloquently, both verbally and in writing. When this chakra is not functioning properly, you may be unable to communicate your emotions, and you may have ear, nose, throat, or dental problems. The aura of this chakra is blue. Blue crystals like turquoise, blue quartz, sodalite, azurite, aquamarine, and lapis lazuli help to stimulate and balance the fifth chakra.

The Sixth Chakra

Also known as the "third eye" chakra, this chakra is located at your forehead, above your brow. When this chakra is in full working order, your intuition and perceptions are keen, your psychic powers are increased, and your creativity is up. When the sixth chakra is unbalanced, you can feel somewhat confused or anxious and you may have eye problems or headaches and/or insomnia. The aura of this chakra is indigo. Indigo-colored crystals like amethyst or sapphire will help this chakra to work well again.

The Seventh Chakra

Also known as the "crown" chakra, it is located at the top of the head. When this chakra is up to its potential, you feel spiritual, highly intuitive, and on the right path to getting where you want to be. When this chakra is not functioning well, you can feel low-spirited or disconnected from the people around you. The aura of this chakra is clear, surrounded by ultraviolet. Good crystals to heal this chakra are diamonds or clear quartz.

The secret to drawing power from crystals is in the focus and concentration. During a magick ritual, George William Russell once said to William Yeats, "You can't evoke great spirits and eat plums at the same time."

Chapter 8

I Ching, the Chinese Oracle

The I Ching, otherwise known as the Chinese Oracle or The Book of Changes, is an ancient method of divination— over 3,000 years old. The I Ching is based on the Tao concepts of yin and yang and works by tuning in to the natural state of flux in the universe. This chapter provides an introduction to I Ching, how it works, and the hexagrams you need to know in order to use I Ching in divination.

The Energy of I Ching

The I Ching is based on the idea that, like the principals of Tao, everything in the universe is in a constant state of movement and flow. In essence, the belief is that nothing happens randomly. When you throw the coins in I Ching, they draw in and pick up on the energy at that moment in time.

This energy is then represented by the combination of lines: yin (broken) and yang (unbroken). So after six throws of the coins, you wind up with one out of sixty-four possible hexagrams, and each has a specific universal meaning attached to it. From this meaning, you can interpret the answer to your question.

Three Coins

Originally, the ancient Chinese practiced I Ching by using bones and, later on, utilizing the stalks of the yarrow plant. Now, I Ching divination is performed with coins. Any coins will work. However, your best option is to use those old Chinese coins with a square hole in the middle.

When you get your coins, make sure you cleanse them, to clear their energy. No ancient Chinese philosopher ever attempted to use the coins with I Ching before they had cleansed and blessed them. Too many people had touched those same coins previously! Remember that energy is transmitted magnetically and is more susceptible to being passed through metal objects—especially personal objects like coins.

In order to accomplish this ritual of cleansing, you can use "smudging" (burning sage or cedar), candles, moonlight, earth (burying them in dirt or sand for twenty-four hours), or water (soaking them in salt water).

The Lines of Yin and Yang

Here is how I Ching divination works. First of all, get out a piece of paper and a pen. Take out the three coins and assign the value of three to one side of the coins and the value of two to the other. (Usually, the side that lists the monetary value of the coin is the "three.") Also designate one side as "heads" and the other as "tails."

- Two is for yin
- Three is for yang

Now, shake all three coins together and concentrate on your question. Drop the coins, and see which are heads and which are tails. Add up the twos and threes, and you should come up with a number that is a six, a seven, an eight, or a nine.

QUESTION?

How should I formulate the question?
In I Ching, avoid asking a simple yes/no question. The question should be about family, work, love, friendship, or making a decision. Here is a sample question to ask: "Why did I make the mistake with ___, and what should I learn from it?"

Throwing for Practice

Let's say that you do your first throw and get two heads and one tails. You've already established that heads are worth two and tails are worth three. That means you've got 2 + 2 + 3 = 7 (the order in which you add up the coins doesn't matter). Now, you translate your resulting number into one of four possible lines, which are listed in **TABLE 8-1**.

Table 8-1 Four Possible Coin Toss Results		
2 + 2 + 2 = 6	moving yin line	—X—
3 + 2 + 2 = 7	yang line	——
3 + 3 + 2 = 8	yin line	— —
3 + 3 + 3 = 9	moving yang line	—O—

On your first toss, you got a 7, an unbroken yang line. On your piece of paper, draw the line. Then, do the coin toss five more times. Each time, add up the values of the three coins and draw the matching line above the previous one (you construct the lines from the bottom up, so that your last line will appear at the top).

Always keep your three coins together, and don't let anyone else touch them. You can have other coins available for when you read for others. Try to store them in something made of earth (for instance, a stoneware jar). Also remember that all three coins must be the same size, shape, and type.

Conversion of Moving Lines

You're not done yet. If you have a circle or an X in your line your hexagram is not finished. You will now need to convert the moving lines (those with an X or a circle in the center) to simple yin and yang lines. This is how it works: A moving yin line becomes a yang line, and a moving yang line becomes a yin line. (If you didn't have any moving lines in your hexagram, you don't need to worry about conversion.)

The next step will be to get the interpretation of the hexagram. Remember: Each line represents the moving and flowing yin and yang energy in nature. All together, the six lines form your hexagram, and there are sixty-four of them, each representing a unique pattern of life.

Interpreting the Hexagrams

The I Ching is one of the best ways to get advice and to understand your current situation better. It is meant to give guidance and advice so you can make the right choices in life. Just like other forms of divination, it has the power to steer you in the right direction, but it cannot provide you with end-all be-all solutions. You'll have to do the work yourself.

To interpret a particular hexagram, first check **FIGURE 8-1** to see which one you've got. Then, refer to the correlating explanations, which follow in numerical order.

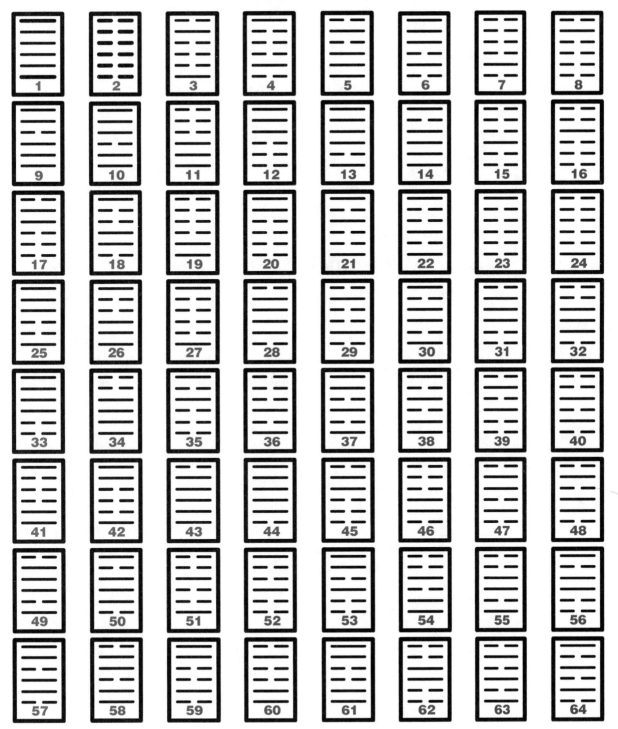

▲ I Ching Quick Chart.

1: CH'IEN, Creative Power

Good energy is strong now, and success is guaranteed if you take advantage of this powerful cycle. Don't waste effort on things that aren't worth your time. Find creative solutions to your problems and act on them without delay. Courage and self-confidence may have been lying dormant before, but now they're in full force. Let go of old arrogance and insecurities that no longer suit you. Be kind, practice humility, and have faith in the future. You're on the right path.

2: K'UN, Yielding and Receiving

The more submissive and responsive you are, the more likely your ideas will take hold and flourish. This is the symbol of earth and of yin energy. It says that you must plant things with patience and they will grow. Seek help from those who are in a position to give you good advice and encourage you without criticism or judgment. Power in this situation will come from your inner strength and will slowly come to fruition. The work you do now will bring you success in the future.

3: CHUN, Difficult Beginnings

Something or someone is testing your patience. If you act quickly or rashly, you will certainly fail. Wisdom comes from learning from the mistakes of others. Gather your information slowly and make decisions with care. Fate will open the door and present you with the right people, opportunities, and situations when you're mentally calm and spiritually ready for it. Expect to have problems and a little chaos at first. Don't worry. What you should be looking at is the big picture and long-term results. Again, perseverance and patience are key here.

4: MENG, Child's Eyes (Inexperience)

You can't do it alone anymore. It may be time to ask for advice and find a friend with a more objective point of view—she can look at your situation in a different light. Is this a repeating problem, situation, or question you have? Things won't change until you've learned from your mistakes and experienced the lesson you need to learn. It may be time to move on. A willingness to change is your only hope of success.

The I Ching should be taken seriously, and is not to be used as a toy. Refrain from asking the same question more than once—you'll only confuse the energy. Instead, take the advice and respect the answer you've been given.

5: HSU, Waiting

Things seem to be delayed right now. They're not moving ahead or where you want them to be. You need to trust that everything will work out the way it should when the time is right. Be content with what you have without forcing the situation. Stifle your doubts, keep your goal in mind, and stay calm. You should also recognize the problem for what it is. Eventually the truth will emerge and your situation will better itself. Don't obsess or overthink things.

6: SUNG, Conflict

This may be a period of conflict and confusion. Do you know what you really want? Things can only be clear when your inner battles are resolved. You also need to hear everyone's side of the story. Only then can you begin to understand the situation fully. Try not to be too judgmental. If someone offers you a take on the situation, you should pay attention. Sudden moves will lead you nowhere. Stay grounded and deal with your inner chaos first.

7: SHIH, Joining Effort

Shih

Only when everyone unites can the problem be solved. The group must have a common goal and only one person in charge. Things done separately should be done for the good of the team. Determination is the key here, but you must be flexible and supportive of other people as well. If you don't let your ego get in the way, you can have a positive outcome.

8: PI, Cooperation

Pi

A united group is one that works well. Are you antisocial? Do you start trouble just to get noticed? You may need to learn how to get along with others better. If you're wondering whether you should join in on something, don't hesitate—your life will be richer for it. Developing friendships and bonds can open new doors in your life. Get involved.

9: HSIAO CH'U, Self-Control

Hsiao Ch'u

By holding back and keeping yourself in check, you can triumph. Remember that the little battles fought and won with fairness are just as important as the big ones. Exercise restraint, humility, and patience. People will see you for who you are and they will respect you for it. Don't seek out momentary satisfaction. Work for what you want and focus on your long-term goals.

10: LU, Tread Carefully

Your ideas should be thought out well before you act on them. There are other forces at work here, so be cautious and polite. Don't step on other people's toes or get in the middle of someone else's business. Stick to what works, throw away what doesn't, and be respectful of others. Don't let a bad mood get the best of you and ruin it for everyone else.

FACT

Each hexagram is made up of two trigrams (three lines). The eight trigrams relate to nature and the symbols of life. They are: KEN (Mountain), K'UN (Earth), SUN (Wind), LI (Fire), CH'IEN (Heaven), TUI (Lake), CHEN (Thunder), and K'AN (Water).

11: TAI, Peace

This is a period of prosperity and contentment. Your ideas are coming to fruition and it's time to start cultivating other projects. Keep doing what you're doing. Opportunities and new contacts will arrive soon, and you must take full advantage of them. Things are moving in the right direction.

12: P'I, Standstill

Things have stopped completely. Why? There is no communication, only confusion. You've reached a point where there is nothing more to do with the situation. If this is the case, don't look to other people who are in no position to help you. Now is the time to rely on yourself and to stand strong. If you can fix the situation, the answer will come to you. If not, you must be prepared for it. Understand the problem and wait for the right time to act.

13: T'UNG JEN, Partnership

Now is a time for joint effort. If everyone works together, the end result will be a success. Don't try to force your opinions on others. If you remain clear and focused on your goal, everyone will eventually see it your way. Be fair and listen to everyone else's point of view. You may have missed something important when you were originally looking at the situation. Keep an open mind.

ALERT!

Always remember that I Ching is an oracle form of divination. It doesn't tell you what will happen; its role is to give you advice that will bring about a positive outcome.

14: TA YU, Abundance

This hexagram speaks of strong inner wealth and, sometimes, of material wealth as well. Your good luck and fortune are on the rise. Projects you started are progressing in the right direction because you've been true to yourself and to others. Relationships you have are important to your growth now. New opportunities are presenting themselves. Appreciate what you have and go with it. Don't let arrogance get in the way of your development.

15: CH'IEN, Humility

By being humble and modest, your good character will shine through and people will recognize your power. In other words, be yourself, and you can be successful in this situation. Remember that being modest doesn't mean that you have to stand back or downplay your talents. Let them show naturally. You don't need to flaunt your achievements—they will speak for themselves.

16: YU, Joyous Anticipation

You've done all the hard work. This is a wonderful time to be contented and to reap all the benefits of what is to come. Don't get lazy, though. You must keep on going the way you were before. In fact, your state of mind now is contagious. If you show your enthusiasm for a project, others will feel the same way about it, too. You are at harmony with the world and the people around you. Use your influences for good.

17: SUI, Being Flexible

If you sense that there is a good leader in this situation, it may be time to follow in his footsteps. If you are that leader, go with it. In order to follow the right path you must develop a new and better way of looking at things. Your old habits will no longer be effective. If you're going to deal with the problem, you must listen to your conscience. Trying to control the situation will get you nowhere. Go slowly, look to the future, and be true to yourself. Others will follow if they sense that you are fair and kind.

18: KU, Neglect

Things are not going your way because you've ignored the heart of the problem for far too long. Because of your indecisiveness, the situation has only become worse. If you want to fix things, you need to get to the root of it and make choices. Constructive and decisive action can lead you to success. Don't blame yourself or others for the situation you're currently in. Forgive all parties involved and move on. There's still time to get on the right track.

19: LIN, Advancement

Finally, you've made progress and things are humming along just fine. Success is close, but you don't need to rush things. Instead, enjoy the process. There are still things that need to be done, but you know exactly what to do. You have the strength now to get things going in the right rhythm. Don't get lazy. Communicate your needs and move ahead with grace. Go with the flow.

20: KUAN, Meditation and Observation

It's time to step back from the situation and get a fresh look at the problem. Be objective about it. Contemplate your next move. Until you understand the situation better, nothing will go the way it should. Luck, intuition, and analysis will aid you. You must be sincere in your purpose. Don't try to manipulate or control things. Don't take everything literally. You have more power in the situation than you realize. Trust yourself and others will, too.

The ancient Chinese philosophy of Tao was established by Lao-tzu. He said, "Follow the nothingness of the Tao and you can be like it, not needing anything, seeing the wonder and the root of everything."

21: SHIH HO, Cutting Through

This problem isn't going to go away by itself. Something needs to be done. You're the only one who can resolve this. The thing is, you have to get to the root of what happened to figure out what to do next. This is the time to take an aggressive approach and tackle the beast, so to speak. Other situations will be resolved once you take care of this, so don't procrastinate.

22: PI, Beauty (Grace)

First impressions count—and so do last ones. If it's not working, walk away with self-respect and grace. If it is, use your charm and influence in order to make the situation work better to your advantage. Real power comes from within. Everyone possesses hidden beauty. Your job is to locate that source and let it shine without fear. Let go of insecurities and arrogance. These things can hold you back from success. Material wealth will not bring you happiness.

23: PO, Splitting Apart

Is there confusion and chaos around you? There's nothing you can do right now to make it better. This is fate working overtime. Everything is breaking apart because it needs to. It's time to get rid of the old way of thinking and bring in the new. Lying low will help you avoid exacerbating the problem. The next cycle is coming up and you need to be prepared for it. Wait, be patient, and don't let it get the best of you.

24: FU, Turning Point

This is a crucial time in your life. Things are starting to happen and a new period is about to start. It's still not time to make a move yet. Understanding will come slowly but surely. You're finally coming out of a rough period. In a way, you're coming back to life. Get ready and reflect on what's happened to you and how much you've changed. You may meet someone very soon who can be a positive influence in your life.

25: WU WANG, Simplicity (Innocence)

If you're true to others, unselfish, and generous with yourself, good intuition will come easily. And you need intuition to make decisions. When choices come from the heart, they're always right, no matter what happens in the end. Trust your hunches and don't be a follower. You know how to deal with the situation. Be confident and creative in your approach.

26: TA CH'U, Taming Power

If you hold back and exercise control, you can gather up strength to use later. Keep still and gather all the information around you. Then, make your move. The world will soon open up to you and you must be ready and at peace with your decisions. Show tenderness, respect, and love to those closest to you.

27: I, Giving Nourishment

This is about making effort where effort is needed: physically, spiritually, mentally, and emotionally. Are you taking care of yourself? Good fortune comes from being in a good place. Eat right, work out if it makes you feel better, relax and don't stress, and communicate with your partner and your family. Don't do things just for the sake of it. Put importance where importance should be placed.

28: TA KUO, Overload

Ta Kuo

Things can't go on the way they've been going. There's too much at stake. You need to take deliberate action based on your knowledge of the situation, not just by your gut. You've gone off the deep end one too many times and it's all coming back now to haunt you. Figure out what you need to concentrate on and let other, less important things go. Success is possible if you can manage your affairs in a more orderly way.

29: K'AN, Dangerous Chasms

K'an

It may feel like you're at the bottom of a hole and still sinking. If you ignore the situation, it could get worse. You may even feel that you're being tested. (You are!) Strength now will come from courage and conviction. Do what you know is right. Even though nothing seems to be working in your favor, things will get better soon. You simply need to remain detached and cool. Don't resist suffering. Learn from it.

In Taoism, the goal of life is balance. Everything has yin and yang energy, positive and negative. According to Lao-tzu, "Beauty and mercy are only recognized by people because they know the opposite, which is ugly and mean."

30: LI, Passionate Adherence

Li

People may regard you as hard-headed in this particular situation. If your stubbornness is coupled with humility, you're making the right moves. Spiritually, we all instinctively know what we need. Sometimes we're dependent on certain things. In this case, it makes sense. Hold on to your beliefs and it will make you stronger. Don't give up what you know to be essential to your happiness.

31: HSIEN, Powerful Attraction

Sometimes you meet someone and things just "click." This is about relationships: business, love, or friendship. The feeling here is mutual. Don't force it. Go with the flow and let things develop when they should. You're forming an incredible bond that is based not just on chemistry but also on mutual respect. Have patience and you'll be successful.

32: HENG, Long-Lasting (Endurance)

This can refer to an excellent marriage, relationship, or long-term project. Things are going well. If they aren't, you only need make a few minor adjustments for everything to return back to the joy you first experienced. This hexagram also indicates that the situation will go well if you stick it out. Don't give up. It's worth hanging on to.

33: TUN, Stepping Back

You've done everything you could. Now is the time to let it go for a while. If it's meant to come back into your life, it will. But you're running up against a brick wall. Try to remain detached and don't let yourself get too vulnerable. An aggressive approach will not work right now. Wait until your luck returns before you make any major decisions.

34: TA CHUANG, Great Fortitude

You have the power, so use it well. Don't take advantage of the situation. Revenge is not the answer. The only reason you've finally reached the place you're in is because you've been good to yourself and have been caring with the people around you. Don't change your character now that you've got the upper hand.

35: CHIN, Moving Ahead

Finally things are going smoothly. You've waited for this to happen for a while, and it's finally on track. Don't doubt too much or wonder why. Have faith in what you're doing and move on ahead. Your ideas are on the mark. People who have been unavailable lately will start popping up now to help you.

36: MING I, Oppression

Why are people ganging up on you? Your ideas are radical. You need to remain focused, be calm, and keep to yourself. Do your own thing. Whether or not they come around should be of no consequence to you. You have to do what you know is right. Don't let others drag you down or damage your sense of self-worth. In the end, you'll come out on top.

37: CHIA JEN, Family

In this case, family discordance is the source of the problem. Are there still some issues you need to work out? It's time to communicate. It may be a good idea to choose someone to mediate the conversation. (Here "family" can also refer to a clan, people you see every day, or someone with whom you live.)

38: K'UEI, Misunderstandings

K'uei

Without trust and tolerance, you won't be able to turn this situation around. If you're having verbal battles, why not give in a little? The phrase "kill them with kindness" seems to apply well here. Try to look at things from someone else's point of view.

39: CHIEN, Removing Obstacles

Chien

This is a difficult situation. You need to look over everything before you make a move. Anyway, the problem is temporary, and you'll come out of it stronger. Stick it out and try to come up with a creative resolution. Make the most of it.

40: HSIEH, Relief

Hsieh

The tension is winding down. Stress and complications are diminishing. It's time to use the creative energy you've been holding within for so long. No one is to blame for the situation you were previously in. Forgive and move on. Things are looking up.

ALERT!

Lao-tzu said, "What is yielding and weak overcomes what is hard and strong. . . . Learn to yield and be soft if you want to survive. Learn to bow and you will stand your full height."

41: SUN, Decrease

This has to do with material expenditures, personally or of a company, or can refer to too much of something in a relationship. The key here is to be conservative. Cut back on your financial spending and spend your time and understanding. It may be frustrating, but eventually you'll be in a position in which you can afford to live the way you want to.

42: I, Increase

You're getting the assistance that you need and things seem to be in your favor. Now may be a good time to expand or to get more serious in your undertakings, relationships, or otherwise. If you've been waiting to make an important decision, do it now. Keep an open mind and your head up, and things will go as planned.

43: KUAI, Dawn (Perseverance)

This is a period to stand resolute and determined. Things will sway to your side if you show everyone that you mean what you say. Just be sure to be direct and not offensive to others involved.

44: KOU, Cautious Meetings

Trust whatever it is your intuition is telling you about the situation. Do things seem too good to be true? Perhaps they are. If there are gatherings or opportunities now to meet new people, go! Be charming, kind, and easygoing. Don't let anyone make you feel the odd man out.

45: TS'UI, Getting Together

Ts'ui

Each group has a leader. If it's you, let your good judgment and fairness shine through. If it isn't, give the chosen leader the respect that she deserves. Harmony and peace come from a team of people who work well together.

46: SHENG, Rising Up

Sheng

Does everything seem too good to be true? Guess what—it's for real. You're in a position now where you can go forward with the situation. If there's still something standing in your way, now is the time to deal with it. Luck and good fortune are on your side.

47: K'UN, Restriction

K'un

Your situation is distressing. You may feel that no matter what you do, something or someone is blocking your way. Accept the reality that things are tough right now and then think of a clever way you can resolve the problem. Take heart that things will get better soon.

48: CHING, Well of Life

Ching

Think of how an old water well worked. People went to it with an empty pail and returned with one full of water. Water is essential to life. In the same way, you must go to the source of your nourishment. Whatever you need, seek it out. Just remember: Getting it from a polluted well is not the answer. Decide whom you can trust before relying on them.

49: KO, Drastic Change

The reason things have happened the way they have is because they had to. You were (or are currently) suffering as a result of a major life lesson you needed to learn. But you're going to come out of this tornado a stronger person. Don't worry—suffering builds character, and you'll soon have a chance to breathe easier.

50: TING, the Cauldron

This period should be about getting nourishment through natural things. Let go of financial worries. Put more importance on feeding your relationships, your spirituality, and your body. Enjoy life, passion, and sincerity.

51: CHEN, Lightning

It strikes in an instant and leaves you feeling confused and shocked. If this is your situation, stand back from it and get your bearings. If you feel this came out of nowhere, search for an answer within. It happened for a reason. Is there something you did to start this chain of events? Don't blame yourself. Fix it.

52: KEN, Staying Still

Instead of letting your emotions take over, analyze why you're letting the situation affect you so strongly. The key is to remain calm and let the complicated moment pass you by. Observe what others are doing in order to get inspiration.

53: CHIEN, Moving Forward

Chien

The key is to let things progress when they will. Fate is playing a role here. Things are going ahead, even if you can't see it with your own eyes. Don't take drastic action right now. You'll soon notice the changes that have been happening around you.

ALERT!

According to Lao-tzu, "Those who always want to be seen will never help others to be. . . . The kind of person who always insists on his way of seeing things can never learn anything from anyone."

54: KUEI MEI, Submissiveness

Kuei mei

This hexagram may refer to a marriage or a relationship in love or business. By letting others take control, you're still keeping the power and force you have within. Sometimes it's necessary to hold back your desires without aggressively pursuing the situation. Let people come to you.

55: FENG, Success

Feng

This is a period of abundance. Don't do anything to stop the flow. Go with it. Projects, ideas, and even relationships are filled with the stuff dreams are made of. It's all within your reach. Luck is on your side.

56: LU, the Nomad

Are you on someone else's turf or unfamiliar ground? Perhaps you're searching for something. If you're feeling out of sorts, make sure to keep both feet on the ground and be yourself. If you act strangely, you'll be treated in a weird way too.

57: SUN, Gentle Force

You don't need to provoke people or to take drastic action in order to get noticed. Actually, strength here comes from exhibiting mildness and inner peace. You can convince someone by holding firm to your convictions. Be gentle, kind, and focused.

58: TUI, Harmony

Happiness and real joy are contagious. When you find beauty or meaning in something, others will see it in the same light. If things are not going well, you know what you need to do. Do it so you can get on the right track again. Get your priorities straight. Success is within your reach.

59: HUAN, Dispersion

Problems now need to be resolved by gentle methods. If you attack, things will get worse. By being open-minded and fair, and by communicating with others, the right solution will come to you. When it does, the problem will seemingly dissolve away.

60: CHIEH, Self-Moderation

Chieh

In order to influence others greatly and really "get under their skin," you need to have a deep understanding of what makes them tick. Careful deliberations you've made will do their work now. Balance is the key here. Move like a cat, slowly and silently.

61: CHUNG FU, Spiritual Truth

Chung Fu

If you're honest with yourself and with others, nothing can go wrong. People will instantly pick up on your sincerity, and will give you what you want. Communicate and speak your mind. Your reservations may be for naught. But don't judge people too quickly—you may have the wrong idea.

FACT

The West had no knowledge of I Ching until the nineteenth century, when a Christian missionary named Richard Wilhelm traveled to China. He was interested in Chinese culture and wisdom, and his Chinese friends taught him about Taoism and I Ching. Over time, Wilhelm was so taken by the philosophic metaphoric guidance of the I Ching that he took it upon himself to translate it from Chinese to English.

62: HSIAO KUO, the Little Things

This is the time to use the little, everyday things as a sort of meditation. Pay attention to what you're doing, and focus. When you can master small things, the big ones will get easier. Now is not the time for action. Don't even think of tackling the major projects or making any big decisions—you're not ready to do that just yet.

63: CHI CHI, Completion

All of your hard work has resulted in success. The project has come full circle. Now is not the time to back off. Keep up the pace and things will continue to go well. You're at a good point in your life right now.

64: WEI CHI, Before Completion

You're almost there. Pressure and stress are high. You have to surpass them and remain focused on your goal. Hard work, determination, and perseverance will aid you. You'll have more tests before you're done. If success seems easy, you're missing something. In the end, however, you'll have what you want.

Chapter 9

The Ancient Magick of Runes

Twenty-five runes compose an ancient alphabet originally used by Germanic and Nordic tribes to make magick, to affect healing, and to communicate with nature. Today, many fortunetellers still use runes in divination, magick, and for the purposes of meditation. All you need is a set of runes (you can make them yourself!), and you'll be ready to make a connection with your future. You can use them for magick, divination, and/or meditation. In this chapter, learn how runes can be your link to the future.

Reading the Secrets

In some ways, runes work like crystals. Although they work in divination, they can also tap into energy and vibrations and can be used for meditation. Simply pick a rune that has an important symbolic meaning for you, hold it in your hand, close your eyes, and take in the positive energy.

In other ways, though, runes are more like the I Ching because they are best used as an oracle. You can ask runes for advice beyond simple yes/no answers. When you are casting runes, your questions should be more involved. For instance, instead of asking, "Should I take this job?" ask, "What will happen if I accept this job?"

ALERT!

The runes will not tell you exactly what you should do. They will speak about the background of the situation. From the answer, though, you'll be able to determine what the next step should be.

Buy or Make Your Own

You can, of course, buy runes at a specialty shop or through the Internet, and you have a variety of different options (and prices) to choose from. However, most psychics advise that you make them yourself. As you create each rune, your energy will be transferred from your hands and into your runes. Once you are done, and are ready for divination, make sure you don't let other people handle your runes for very long at any one time.

Most psychics agree that the time it takes to do a reading for another will not alter the energy of the runes. Plus, you can always cleanse them with candles, salt water, earth, or the moon. Just make sure not to lend them to anyone. Do the reading and then put them away.

Make your runes from a natural material. You can use stones worn smooth by sand or weather or carve them from wood (if you take the wood from a living tree, make sure to say a little prayer before you do so). You can also make your runes out of clay. In the past, bones were used as well, but this practice is no longer encouraged because of the energy remaining within these objects, which were once part of living creatures.

After you've chosen the material and have the little round objects ready, carve or paint each rune's symbol on one side and leave the other side blank. Make sure there are no identifying marks on the "blank" side and that all the runes are uniform in shape and weight. You don't want to know which rune you're looking at before you flip it over!

You will also need a pouch where you can keep your runes when you are not using them. Make sure the pouch is made of natural material like fur, cotton, linen, or hemp. You'll also need a "casting cloth," used to wrap up the runes and during casting, so that they are kept clean. Any natural material will do, as long as it's white or ivory on one side—this light, neutral color is necessary for keeping the energy unbiased.

The Runic Alphabet

There are actually many different versions of runes. In this book, you will get an introduction to The Elder Futhark, the most well-known and the oldest runic alphabet in existence, used many centuries ago by ancient German and Scandinavian tribes. The term "futhark" comes from the first six letters of the Runic alphabet: f, u, th, a, r, and k.

The Elder Futhark only used twenty-four runes (the twenty-fifth rune that we have in divination is left blank on both sides). The twenty-four runes may be divided into three groups of eight letters. These three levels are referred to as the three *aettir* (the plural for *aett):*

First Aett: F, U, Th, A, R, K, G, W
Second Aett: H, N, I, J, Y, P, Z, S
Third Aett: T, B, E, M, L, Ng, D, O

Each of these letters has a runic symbol to identify it.

Interpreting the Symbols

Here are the interpretations of each rune, organized by the aett to which it belongs. Note that the aettir are named after the Norse deities Freya, Heimdall, and Tyr.

The First Aett

The first aett is also known as Freya's aett. Freya is the goddess of love and fertility. Consequently, this aett concerns itself with matters of creation—love, happiness, and life.

Fehu

This rune, which literally means "cattle," refers to worldly, spiritual, and material possessions. In terms of meditation, it refers to abundance, fertility, nurturing, good health, life force, and wealth. In divination, it reminds you to be content with, nourish, and protect what you already have. You need to share with others. Don't be stingy with your love. Financial gain is possible. Your relationship needs to be looked at more closely.

Uruz

This rune, which means "wild ox," is similar to Fehu, but it refers to the untamed, unruly side of it. It also speaks of strength, power, instinct, sexuality, and passion. In divination, it says that something important is just beginning or, instead, coming to an end. If it is the latter, good things will come of it later. When you pull this rune, it also means luck and fortune in relationships and career. It advises you to be focused and to be above the pettiness of others. Beware of others controlling or manipulating you for their own gain.

Thurisaz

Translated as "giant," this rune refers to the great hammer of Thor, the god of protection. Thurisaz represents luck, protection, introspection, and knowledge. In divination, it means that you must prioritize your goals and then put all your efforts toward the most important cause. Hardship should be expected. Someone behind the scenes, unbeknownst to you, is helping you. Thurisaz can also be used in meditation as protection against negative people and situations.

ALERT!

Thurisaz warns that powerful forces are involved in your situation. Study the surrounding runes to determine whether this rune is speaking of love, career, or family.

Ansuz

This rune signifies "mouth," and it speaks of communication, taking advice, and the connection between mind and spirit. In divination, it says that you will receive messages through others. Keep your eyes and ears open to wisdom transmitted through everyday occurrences. Expect the unexpected. In meditation, use Ansuz for creative inspiration.

Raidho

This rune may be translated as "wagon" or "chariot" and refers to movement. In divination, it means it's a good time to get away, to travel. It can also mean that it's time for you, spiritually, to let go and move on. It also warns about a chance to clear things up with people from your past that you will run into soon. Last, Raidho may signal a positive move or change of living location.

Kenaz

Meaning "torch," this rune refers to the element of fire and represents love and the birth of inspiration, creativity, and enlightenment. In divination it can mean gifts or loss, depending on the surrounding runes. In a relationship, it says that both sides are valid—you should listen to each other. It also warns that good changes are coming and that you should be prepared for them.

If you draw the rune Kenaz along with Ansuz at the same time, it indicates that there are very powerful forces at work here. It could mean that a relationship is about to change drastically or that a seemingly simple gesture someone makes means much more than you can imagine.

Gifu

This rune, which signifies "gift," refers to love and generosity. This rune always has a positive meaning. In divination, it can mean that a wedding is on the horizon or that a relationship will be taken to the next level. It can also point to good fortune on the way in career or business. Partnerships and relationships can be beneficial to you now. If you are single, it could indicate a new romance.

Wunjo

This rune, "joy," is a positive indication that good things are ahead. In divination, this rune can represent success or reward for your achievements and hard work, or instant clarification on matters that were previously difficult to discern. Look at the surrounding runes to see if the source of contentment is from love, career, or life in general. In romance, it could mean a deepening of affection or a harmonious relationship.

The Second Aett

The second aett is also known as the aett of Heimdall, the warden of the Norse gods, who held the keys to the heavens. According to certain myths, Heimdall was in charge of letting souls into heaven, and perhaps that is why the second aett has to do with transformation, whether in career, fortune, money, or achievements.

Hagall

This rune means "hail" and refers to the things over which you have no power. It speaks of delays, problems, loss, or major changes that are part of fate. If you get Hagall during divination, the runes are telling you that you are learning a karmic lesson. The best thing to do is accept your defeat and learn from your suffering. In the end, you'll have a clearer idea of the path you need to take. You're being tested, so handle it gracefully.

Nyd

This rune, translated as "need," reminds you about the constraints you are facing because of things you cannot do without. It is similar to Hagall in that it also refers to delays, problems, and a life lesson you need to experience. Though there are obstacles and much frustration in your way, there's not much you can do about it. Keep your head up and try to get through it. In relationships, Nyd represents possessiveness, jealousy, and too many one-sided rules.

Isa

Isa means "ice," and like Hagall and Nyd, it refers to delays. Things seem to be "frozen" right now and you'll just have to wait it out. In divination, this could be referring to a romance that's slowed down, if not stopped altogether. This is not a time to make any major changes or to use an aggressive approach. It's downtime. Use it wisely and don't feel sorry for yourself. Also, watch out for double-crossing or insincere friends.

Jera

This is a "harvest" rune and reminds you that you reap what you sow. If you work hard, you'll soon begin to feel the results. In divination, it could also refer to the end of something—a job, a friendship, or a love relationship. Just know that with this ending comes a new period, and that it's all for the better.

Eihwaz

Eihwaz, or "yew," refers to a particular tree that was essential to the ancient Germanic tribes. They used this tree to make weapons as well as magickal items. In divination, this rune warns that you must protect yourself against foreseeable problems of the future. Fear can only hold you back. When you draw this rune, it is a warning to fix disaster before it happens. If you heed this advice, you'll be victorious.

FACT

Legend has it that the Norse god named Odin was the one who first invented and discovered runes. According to mythology, Odin went up the World Tree and hung suspended for nine days. At the end of that time, he harnessed the energy of the universe and presented the world with his gift: the runes.

Perdhro

This rune is "secret" or "mystery," the rune of occult powers, instinct, magick, destiny, and fate. In divination, when you pull this rune, it could mean that you'll have an important epiphany soon and that you should trust your instinct with it. Although this is a "fate" rune, it also says to act now; you can change things so they'll go the way you want them to.

Elhaz

This rune means "elk" and deals with protection, instinct, and the path between the subconscious mind and the world. In divination, pulling this rune means you can expect surprises. Elhaz may also act as a warning not to get too emotional regarding the situation you're currently in. You can prevent disaster by looking at the truth more objectively and with a clear head.

Sygel

This is the "sun" rune, and it refers to light coming back into your life. In divination, expect a secret to be revealed—or perhaps a matter of importance will come to light and you'll know how to deal with it. Sygel is a positive rune and predicts good fortune. If things aren't going the way you'd hoped, this rune says you should face the problem and conquer it.

The Third Aett

The third aett is Tyr's aett, named for the Norse god of battle. The runes in this aett relate to matters of spiritual reformation as well as mental growth.

Tyr

This rune carries the name of Tyr, and refers to strength, bravery, emotional pain, and discipline. A good warrior always handles problems right away. In divination, this means you need to conquer your fear in the situation in order to come out as a winner. The truth is always the best route. Don't try to control things or they will turn around and control you.

Beorc

This rune is the birch; it refers to family, rebirth, fertility, and the mother of all living things. In divination, it indicates something joyous happening within the family—a wedding, a new birth, pregnancy, or good news of a child's or parent's accomplishments. This rune also brings luck to the querent in terms of a new romance or a new job offering. Finally, Beorc indicates spiritual and mental cleansing—clarifying new ideas and getting rid of old ones.

Ehwaz

This rune, which signifies "horse," refers to progress, movement, change, and clearing the obstacles in your path. In divination, it could signal a change of address. It could also refer to a positive reunion with an old friend or family member. Ehwaz does not refer to immediate changes—they happen gradually and with some help. If your question has to do with whether you can trust someone, the answer is yes. If the problem has to do with sexuality, this rune indicates that, with determination, everything will be solved.

ALERT!

If you pull the rune Ehwaz and it comes out near the rune Nyd, it could be referring to friendships and family. The message is that right now you need to surround yourself with people you trust and who are unselfish and generous with you—those who will tell you the truth even if it hurts.

Mannaz

This rune means "human being" or "mankind"; it refers to everything that holds us above all other animals: our ability to rationalize, communicate complex thoughts, and intellectualize. In divination, Mannaz reminds you to stay grounded, think things through, and make your decision based on logic and experience instead of deciding on a whim. It also says that help is on the way.

Lagaz

This is a "water" rune, a rune of nature. Lagaz has to do with revelations, intuition, and things that move and change without your control. When you pull this rune, it indicates that you might be trying to manipulate your situation too much. You need to go with the flow, as long as you know what is right. Luck is on your side now. Like flowing water, the problem will move on. Be honest with yourself and accept what's happening. Don't punish yourself.

Ing

This rune is named after the god of fertility and points to success, luck, and good fortune. In divination, this rune warns that although you may have to go through some hardships and have some difficulties, you'll be victorious in the end. It also represents giving birth to new ideas or new situations that will be beneficial to you. Stop dwelling in the past; the future is looking bright and has much to offer you.

Daeg

This is the rune of light and enlightenment; it deals with spiritual growth, positive guiding forces, and finding your strength within. In divination, this is a powerful rune that brings you luck. If you have an open mind and look at the positive side of things, nothing can go wrong. This rune cancels out any negative aspects of runes surrounding it.

Othel

The rune of property and possessions, Othel may refer to inheritance (whether financial, genetic, or otherwise). In divination, this rune can be positive or negative. It could mean that you're holding on to love or money too tightly. It could also signify that you need to get back to family values or that you're too constricted by them and you should open up more. Studying the surrounding runes will help you understand specifically what this rune is referring to.

Wyrd

Wyrd is a blank rune that was not originally in the runic alphabet. In divination, it is used as a "wild card" and has to do with fate, karma, and destiny. Paired with other runes, it automatically says that there are other forces at work on your situation over which you have no control. It may also mean that the outcome of this situation is not yet determined and hinges solely on how you handle yourself with it. Wyrd also indicates the unexpected or a surprise.

If you cast the runes and Othel appears next to Gifu, you will definitely have money coming in soon from family or even an unexpected source. If Othel is near the rune Lagaz, it says that a current dream about family or someone close to you should be regarded as prophecy.

Casting Runes

There are many different ways to cast your runes. You can even use the spreads done for Tarot cards (Chapter 6). Use three runes to do past, present, and future. Or, pick one rune before you start your day to see how things will go.

You can pick the runes directly out of the bag or spread them all out face-down on your casting cloth and guide your hand over them to feel the energy, picking up the runes one at a time. Another strategy is to shake the rune pouch and then cast the runes over the casting cloth. The runes that appear face up will have something to tell you about the question you have.

You can make up your own spreads by assigning different values to each rune placement. For example, if you create a spread of six runes, determine ahead of time that the first rune will relate to the background of the problem, the second to obstacles in the way, the third to how others view the problem, the fourth to advice and guidance, the fifth to handling the advice, and the sixth to the outcome. Create your own rune layouts—it will make divination by runes more personally meaningful.

ALERT!

When creating your own spreads, it's important to be consistent. Don't change your mind midway according to which rune you've picked. It will help to write down the spread you've chosen before you cast. That way, there will be no debate as to your response to the question.

Take seriously the advice you receive from the runes. If you ask the same question twice in one day, or even in the same week, you're going to get a confused response. You can make your question more specific, but if you're getting an answer that doesn't fit the question or, perhaps, one you don't want, keep it in mind and leave it alone. Nothing good will come out of stressing the energy—and yourself. Ⓔ

Chapter 10

The Future Is in Your Hands

You probably know that each person's fingerprints are unique—but what about the lines and markings found on the palm? Do they carry any special information? In fact, they do. Palm markings hold clues to your past, your present, and your future, as well as clues about your personality, attitudes, and resolve, which add up to give you an idea of what lies ahead.

Introducing Palm Reading

Palmistry was first practiced in ancient China and India, where it appeared over 3,000 years ago. Like other forms of divination, it originally had other uses—ancient sages used palm reading to make character and personality assessments and to provide counseling. Some professional palm readers still use this method today.

Just about anyone can learn how to read palms—you don't even need to have psychic ability or powerful intuitive skills. Once you learn the combinations of lines, sections of the hand, and other essential details, you can read any hand (including your own) and make a valid interpretation. And when you start getting good and have some experience, you might even come up with a few new theories of your own.

In any form of divination, what you are doing is looking for trends and patterns. After analyzing a number of hands, you might notice a marking that people of similar character or personality have in common. If so, you're on to a trend—don't be afraid to use this information the next time you see it!

The most important thing to remember about palmistry is that, like other forms of divination, it's meant to show you opportunities and possibilities available to you in your lifetime. It won't tell you exactly the way things are supposed to go. In fact, all professional hand analyzers agree that the lines in your hand change according to life decisions *you* make along the way. Remember free will? We make our own destiny.

Palm readers will tell you that different markings can be noted in as little as two or three months—and some even believe that the patterns of your hands may change in minutes! For this reason, it may be a good idea to make a photocopy or an ink print of your palm once a year, so that you can compare the changes that may appear over time.

Seven Hand Shapes

Begin the reading by examining the shape of your hand. There are seven major hand shapes, and each one will give you information about your personality, character, likes and dislikes, and hidden talents.

1. **The artistic hand:** The artistic hand, also known as the conic or pear-shaped hand, looks strong and has long fingers that are pointed (narrowed) at the ends. People with artistic hands tend to follow their instincts. They are creative, expressive, somewhat moody, and at times are overly sensitive to criticism.

2. **The romantic hand:** Also known as the psychic hand, this type of hand is very long, delicate, and graceful. People with psychic hands usually have vivid imagination, are intuitive, and love fantasy more than reality, so they may be overly idealistic.

3. **The pragmatic hand:** This type of hand has a square-shaped palm and thick, rounded fingers. People with pragmatic hands tend to be stubborn—nonconformists who aren't always politically correct. They tend to have no tact and sometimes, albeit unintentionally, can hurt other people's feelings. The pragmatists are also very traditional and don't change much throughout life.

4. **The philosophic hand:** A thick, wide hand with fingers swelling at the joints (the points where they bend). Philosophic hands often belong to kind people who are loners. They tend to intellectualize everything and are ruled by the head and not by the heart. Sometimes, they are overly wary of others and their intentions.

5. **The Renaissance hand:** A combination of two or more of the other categories. Renaissance hands belong to enigmatic people who are a contrast of personalities. These people are often good at a number of different things and may, for instance, be pragmatic and artistic at the same time.

6. **The independent hand:** A long palm with long, tapering fingers. People with independent hands are always on the go and love to travel. They generally dislike overanalyzing and prefer action to contemplation.

7. **The basic hand:** A thick, wide palm with short, blunt fingers. Basic-handed people often work hard and are trustworthy, if not a little dull

and overly practical—they probably won't ever be mistaken for social butterflies. Although these people may be intelligent, they are rarely street smart.

If you are doing a reading for someone else, begin your reading with a handshake—you'd be surprised what you can learn from a simple handshake, as long as you pay attention. The firmness and the duration of the handshake should provide you with some clues about the handshaker's personality.

At Your Fingertips

Once you've examined the shape of the hand, turn your attention to the fingers. First, examine the fingertips—are they square, rounded, pointed, or mixed? (Be sure you are looking at the fingertips and not at the fingernails.)

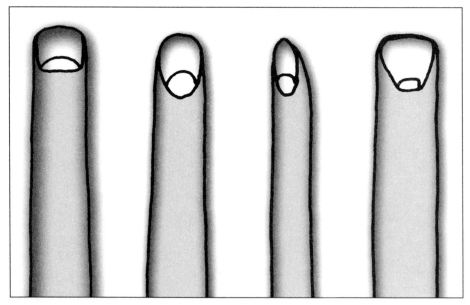

▲ Square, rounded, pointed, and mixed fingertips.

1. **Square fingertips:** You like to remain grounded and prefer to surround yourself with tranquil people who won't disturb you too much or ask too many questions. You are probably a hard worker and have a good head for business and for managing money.

2. **Rounded fingertips:** If you have rounded fingertips, you understand the world around you and are very good at giving advice. You are a sympathetic, caring individual who will fight for a good cause and usually likes to take the side of the underdog. You are loyal and proud; you don't seek revenge and tend to forgive easily—but not forget it. You can be quite romantic and love music and food.

3. **Pointed fingertips:** These point to a person who can, at times, be fastidious in his or her projects and undertakings. If you have pointed fingers, beware of being somewhat paranoid—it is often unwarranted. You are a good communicator and like to discuss various subjects, all of which you are quite knowledgeable about. It's possible that you have an active interest in politics and/or charity events. In general, pointed-finger people are very visual, and some have a photographic memory.

Much of palmistry is common logic. While doing a reading, press your client's palm. If it is hard or firm, it indicates a strong, hard disposition; a softer or cushiony palm indicates a person who is more spontaneous and easygoing.

4. **Mixed (spatulate) fingertips:** If your fingertips are square at the top but rounded on the sides, they indicate that you are a person who waits until the last minute to do something, and then does it exceedingly well. You are an adventurous person who doesn't feel the need to stay close to home but can be equally content doing so. People like you gravitate toward other outgoing, bright, sunny types and usually don't settle down until they meet their soul mate. As a result, they marry at a later age than most.

Finger Lengths

In addition to the fingertips, also look at the fingers themselves, noting their shape and length. If your fingers are all basically the same length, you are an easygoing person who is stable; someone people know they can count on. The same is true if your fingers are stubby.

Most of the time, however, some of your fingers will be longer than the others:

- If your thumb is quite long, it means that you're not a follower; you march to the beat of your own drum.
- If your index finger is as long as your third finger, it means you can be overly proud yet sensitive about it. You are also a person who likes to win.
- If your middle finger is much longer than the other fingers, it means that you sometimes take things too literally and you may want to think about lightening up a little.
- If your third finger is as long as your middle finger, it means that you enjoy spending time by yourself and that you have a quick wit and an intelligent mind.
- If your little finger (pinkie) is much shorter than the rest of your fingers, it means that you are stubborn but charming and you usually get your way. If it's quite long, it means that you can be a good communicator when you already have in mind what you want to say; extemporaneous speaking is not your strong suit.

Also look at the shape of your fingers. If your index finger is bent toward your middle finger, it means that you are never truly happy without a big love in your life. If your third finger is bent, it means you may experience deep suffering for love or family issues.

QUESTION?

Which hand should I read?
Some palmists read the dominant hand (that is, if you are right-handed, read the right one). Others maintain that you should read both. Your dominant hand shows your life as it is now, and your other hand shows all your unrealized potential.

The Major Lines

Now that you've examined your hands and fingers, it's time to look at the lines that appear on your palm. Of all the possible lines and markings that you may see, you are sure to have three major lines that you share in common with most humans—your life line, head line, and heart line. Most professional hand analyzers agree that you should examine these lines first, before you go on to look at other palm lines, palm mounts, and other markings.

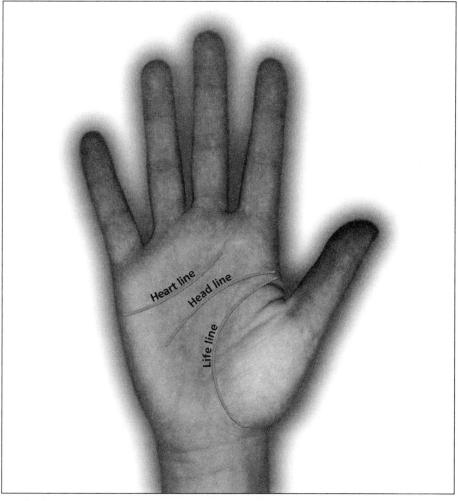

▲ Life, head, and heart lines.

The Life Line

Years ago, palm readers would read this line to determine how long you would live. However, modern readers now believe that such an interpretation is overly simplistic and absurd. Rather than life duration, your life line establishes your life force. If your life line is heavy and long, without many creases or breaks, you have a strong life force—that is, you will have a relatively easy life and an opportunity to make the most of it, living it to the fullest.

As you examine your life line, here is what you should be looking for:

- If your life line veers toward the thumb, it's likely that you find comfort in your family and prefer to stay close to home.
- If another line runs over your life line, you have a protective spirit or angel guiding and helping you in life.
- If your life line has many breaks, you may have a few major turning points in your lifetime, such as a completely new career change or a divorce and second marriage.
- Two life lines that eventually join into one signal some sort of devastating childhood experience that has caused you to lose touch with your true nature. The point where the lines meet represents the time when you finally dealt with your past and have regained your peace and balance.

ALERT!

Someone with a "short" life line can live a full, healthy, wonderful life, just as a person with a long life line can. People with a shorter life line may just have to work a little harder at it.

The Head Line

The head line deals with your intellect, mind, character, and career possibilities. The darker and more pronounced the head line is on the palm, the more analytical and intellectual you are. If the head line is a faint, thin line, you may experience emotional struggles through life and may be quite sensitive to the callous words of others.

Also check to see if your head line slants. If it runs straight across the hand, you are a good leader who is strict but fair. If it slants downward, you have creative and artistic vision. However, a slanted line may also indicate moodiness and capriciousness. If your head line droops severely, you may have a neurotic or anxious personality.

In certain cases, the head line may intersect the life line, which indicates fear of relationships because you are afraid of getting hurt, as you may have been hurt during your childhood.

The Heart Line

The heart line relates to anything concerning love, romance, and relationships of all kinds. It can refer to emotions, strength, sensitivity, and dealing with all matters of the heart. In general, palmistry dictates that people who have a strong, deeply etched heart line pointing toward the index finger will have a happy and satisfying marriage. If your heart line goes toward the middle finger, you need to have the upper hand in your relationships, even if you may appear to be the less dominant one.

If you have a weak heart line that is broken up into sections, you may have relationship or love problems. Whether or not you deal with those setbacks and fight for what you want remains up to you. If the line contains many smaller lines that branch off of it, you are flirtatious and have a tendency toward infidelity (even though you may never act upon it).

Just as with the head line, note the general course of your heart line. If it runs straight across the hand, you are probably one of those people who like to get straight to the point in love, don't like a lot of flowery talk from their partner, and hate deceit. If your line curves radically downward, you want to be needed, wanted, and cared for, even if you are an independent person.

If your heart line begins very high up on the hand, close to the little finger, you may be selling yourself short and don't know your own worth. Don't worry—you'll bloom as soon as you let go of other people's expectations and live life the way you feel you should. Beware of being uptight and/or emotionally (or sexually) cold and withdrawn. If, on the other hand, your heart line is placed very low on your palm, you may have problems being in a monogamous relationship.

If your heart line touches the head line, you were previously guided completely by the heart and by instinct, but at the point where the lines touch, you've changed to become more level-headed and rational about your dealings with love. You may still be optimistic, but now you're also more cautious.

Clues in Other Lines

Other important lines include the Mercury line, Apollo line, and Saturn line, named after the Roman gods Mercury (messenger), Apollo (the sun god), and Saturn (the god of agriculture and the father of Jupiter, the king of the Roman gods).

Mercury Line

Also known as the health line, the Mercury line deals with matters of health, constitution, and stamina, showing your natural health tendencies—whether you are likely to be riddled with illness in life or to have overall good health. If you have a strong, well-defined line, you should have no problems with your health, as long as you take good care of yourself. If the line is very pronounced, you may have healing powers.

Saturn Line

Also known as the fate line, the Saturn line has to do with luck and also represents your career and accomplishments. If you have a long fate line, you almost always land on your feet. If it moves straight up, your path has been chosen for you and you should have a smooth ride ahead. If your fate line intersects the life line at some point, you will have a lot of support from a family member or someone else who is emotionally close.

Apollo Line

Also known as the fortune line, the Apollo line deals with money and finances. If your Apollo line is deeply etched, you will have a nice income that will allow you to live comfortably. If this line is broken up into parts, you may have some problems with earning money or keeping what you've already got.

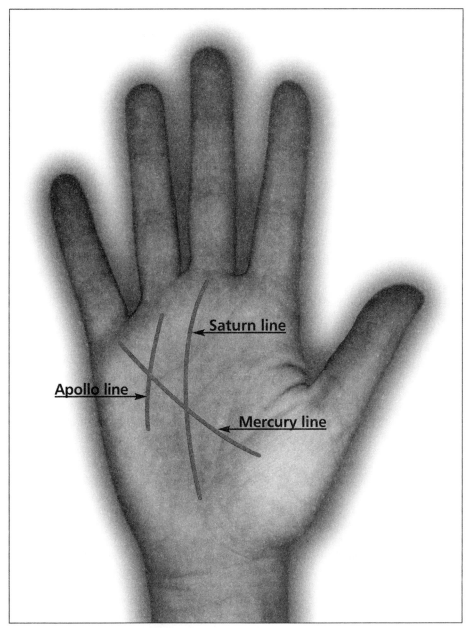

▲ Mercury, Apollo, and Saturn lines.

Marriage and Children

In the upper corner of your palm, underneath your pinky, you may have one or more horizontal lines that come from the edge of your palm. These are your marriage lines. Each one represents a long-term relationship or a marriage (the length determines how long the relationship will last). These lines don't always appear right away—if you don't have any, you may still get them in the future.

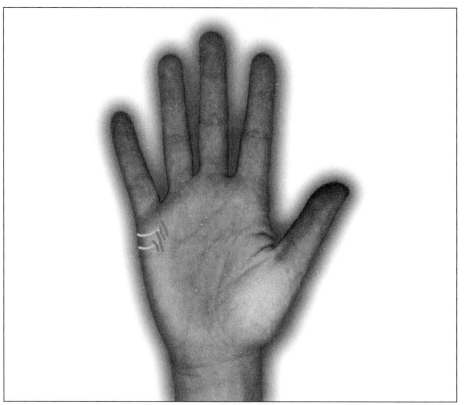

▲ Marriage and child lines.

ALERT!

The validity of marriage lines is debatable. Many modern palm readers agree that it's very difficult to predict when or if someone will marry. Only use this method if it works for you. The same applies to reading child lines.

The vertical lines that branch off the marriage lines are believed to be child lines. In the old days, palmists determined whether a child would be a boy or girl based on the depth and clarity of these markings (deeper ones for boys and lighter ones for girls). Today, palm readers will tell you that child lines don't necessarily represent your own kids—they may symbolize other children who are close to you, whether they are nephews and nieces, adoptive or foster children, or even students (if you're a teacher).

Reading Hand Mounts

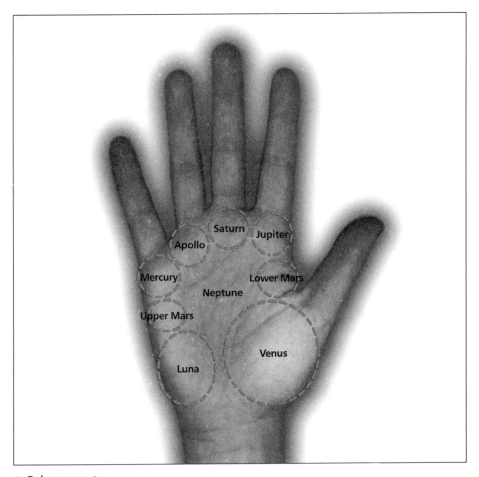

▲ Palm mounts.

In addition to reading lines, palmists usually check the palm mounts—small mounts of flesh located at specific parts of the palm. The key is to look at a palm laid out horizontally, so that you can see which of the mounts are more or less pronounced than others.

1. **Mount of Mercury:** A pronounced Mercury mount indicates that you manage your money well. In fact, you are probably very lucky when it comes to finances. Often, people with a large Mercury mount are also blessed with good communication skills.

2. **Mount of Apollo:** This mount indicates talent in music, design, or other creative endeavors. If you have a large Apollo mount, chances are good that you can achieve fame or recognition—as long as you develop your talents.

3. **Mount of Saturn:** A large Saturn mount may warn that you have a tendency for depression and exhibit what is known as an artistic personality—you are very instinctive, sometimes moody, and are said to possess a rather bohemian or earthy nature.

4. **Mount of Jupiter:** The Mount of Jupiter is the mount of success. If your Jupiter mount is well-developed, you can be successful in anything you choose to do. However, the danger is that you also have an overdeveloped ego and too much pride; many of these people enjoy showing off their material possessions or have a thirst for power.

5. **Mount of Upper Mars:** A well-developed Mount of Upper Mars indicates that you are somewhat confrontational. You are especially competitive when playing games or participating in sports.

6. **Mount of Lower Mars:** Just as with the Mount of Upper Mars, if your Lower Mars mount is overdeveloped, you may have a too-confrontational and even combative personality.

7. **Mount of Neptune:** Because it is located in the center of the palm, the Neptune mount is rarely larger (that is, higher) than other palm mounts. However, a thickly padded Neptune indicates charisma; if a deep crease runs through this mount, you may have trouble seeing within yourself to find the answers you need.

8. **Mount of Luna:** The Luna mount is symbolic of imagination, intuition, and creativity. The well-developed Mount of Luna shows a vivid imagination and a passion for nature, travel, poetry, art, and literature.

9. **Mount of Venus:** If you have a large Venus mount, you know how to love deeply and have a generous nature. There is a definite possibility that you will find great happiness in romantic and creative pursuits.

Chapter 11

What the Numbers Hold in Store

Divining the future with the help of numbers is an old practice that has been around for thousands of years. In this chapter, find out how you can better understand your life's purpose by figuring out your life path or destiny number, karma number, soul number, identity number, spiritual force number, and your personal year number. These numbers will help you see where your life is now and where you're headed. You can even use numbers to help you in love.

The Basics of Numerology

The beauty of numerology is that anyone can do it—all you need is a pen, paper, and just a few simple calculations. Numerology, like other divination methods, taps into the constantly moving and magnetic energy of the universe. Since your soul is one part of these intricate workings, numbers are just symbols that help you to translate who you are in relation to the world around you.

Every person has many different numbers that work as codes. When these numbers are deciphered, you can learn about your karma, destiny, personality, and spiritual and emotional influences. You can even discover why some people (with opposing numbers to your own) may get on your nerves, though you've never been able to figure out why.

Ancient Origins

Numerology, also known as "arithomancy" or "numeromancy," has very murky origins. Many ancient cultures, including the ancient Egyptians and the Babylonians, were said to have held strong beliefs in the power of numbers as devices used to discover certain mysteries of the future. The Mayans, whose civilization dates back to 2000 B.C., also had a complete and complex number system, which they used to make predictions as well as astronomical and mathematical calculations.

And, of course, there was the Father of Mathematics, the famous Greek philosopher and mathematician Pythagoras, who lived some 2,600 years ago. Pythagoras believed that all concepts and consequences in life and in the universe could be expressed and rationalized with numbers. He devoted most of his life to breaking down the codes and how they related to the world in general.

ALERT!

Your spiritual numbers will help you determine where you are in your life, and where you're going. In order to calculate each number, you follow a specific formula and then add up the digits until you get a single-digit number between 1 and 9.

Life Path Number

The life path number is your destiny number; it may best be described as the goal that your soul is striving for in this lifetime. Which life path number is yours? You calculate it based on your date of birth. Let's use the fictional birth date of January 4, 1968, as an example. First, convert the month into a digit. January is the first month, so you change it to 1; February is a 2, March a 3, and so on, until you get to December, which converts to 12 (or 1 + 2).

Next, add all the digits together: 1 + 4 + 1 + 9 + 6 + 8 = 29. Keep adding the digits together until you get a single-digit number: 2 + 9 = 11; 1 + 1 = 2. Your result, 2, is your life path number.

Here are the interpretations for each of the life path numbers:

1: Your soul wants to be ambitious, and in fact it is highly motivated and strong, but also a little pushy. You are a natural leader, and if you've already attained a position of leadership, you're on the right track. If not, work toward your goal—it's something you can definitely achieve.

2: Whether or not you realize it, your soul is striving to be loved, understood, respected, and maybe even coddled. It's time to get rid of negative influences around you, even if they happen to come from members of your family. Stop judging people. Instead, accept the people whose company you enjoy, no matter who they are. Be good to them and they'll, in turn, be good to you.

3: You need to somehow combine the artistic and creative part of your life with your career and romance, even though it may be difficult.

4: Your soul wants you to learn how to make more balanced decisions based on the future, not on the present, and on your life as a whole, not a particular aspect. If your whole life is centered on romance, for example, maybe it's time that you paid more attention to where the rest of your life is moving.

5: You need to stop being so critical of yourself. Your soul wants to be free. Stop looking enviously at what others have. Material possessions do not equal happiness.

6: You have a strong desire for a long-lasting relationship, but you won't settle down with someone not right for you. Don't worry! You are right to stick to your convictions.

7: Your soul wants to protect itself by creating its own power cocoon. You're worried that if you stop believing that you're capable and strong, people will lose faith in you. Look to others for help—it won't hurt.

8: You want so much to be successful in work that you don't always see the big picture. Contentment comes from balance. You can have it all: work, love, family, travel. If your career has been disappointing to you so far, why are you still holding on? Maybe it's time for a big change.

9: You've evolved way past most other people. Sometimes, though, it's better to be a little superficial and give your brain a rest. You don't have to be "tuned in" all of the time.

Karma Number

Your karma number is a "feel good" number that will bring you luck and take you on the right path. Calculate your karma number by using the letters in your everyday name (not necessarily the name you received at birth). If, for example, the name on your birth certificate is Winifred Alice Lee but everyone calls you Freddy Stanton, use the latter one.

As an example, let's take the name Freddy Lee. To figure out this name's karmic number, write out the letters of the name and give each letter a numerical value (refer to **TABLE 11-1** to get the numerical values of letters): F = 6, R = 9, E = 5, D = 4, D = 4, Y = 7, L = 3, E = 5, E = 5. Add up these values: 6 + 9 + 5 + 4 + 4 + 7 + 3 + 5 + 5 = 48. Keep adding up the digits until you get a single-digit number: 4 + 8 = 12; 1 + 2 = 3. So Freddy Lee's karmic number is 3.

TABLE 11-1 NUMERICAL VALUES OF LETTERS

1	2	3	4	5	6	7	8	9
A	B	C	D	E	F	G	H	I
J	K	L	M	N	O	P	Q	R
S	T	U	V	W	X	Y	Z	–

If you use your middle name or initial in everyday situations, you can include it in the calculation of your karma number. If, however, your name includes "Jr." or "Sr.," always leave them out. These are titles and should not be figured into the equation.

Here is what each karma number means:

1. Have you ever been drawn to this number? Try it out while playing the lottery or for doing simple things in everyday life. This number is connected with you.

2. You very much want to bond with certain people in your life but, sometimes, you have difficulty doing so. The key is to stop trying to imagine and guess what the other person wants. You need to do and say what comes from the heart. The person who recognizes your sincerity will be more drawn to you.

3. How did you get so lucky? Things work out for you, don't they? This is a very powerful karma number, though it doesn't always work in romance. You like to shake things up a little and let people see the provocative side of you, which is fine, as long as you remain grounded.

4. Luck sometimes doesn't fall your way because you analyze things to death. Instead of being so practical all of the time, why not try following your instinct once in a while? It will do you good. On the other hand, you've survived some scams that others have fallen victim to because of your solid-based nature. The key is to find a balance between going with your heart and going with your head.

5. Your luck is especially strong when you're in foreign countries or strange situations. You also have a good sense of direction and you have good luck with cars, airplanes, and other modes of transportation.

6. You have good family karma. Though you may have had problems in your childhood, your family supports you now. Consequently, you have to work less to prove yourself to them.

7. Luck is on your side when it comes to contacts for work or for romance. Most of your relationships will come out of introductions from others you know.

8. Your luck lies in work, finance, and money matters. If you aren't seeing any positive results, you're doing something wrong. Try solving your problems at home first. Soon after, your work issues will fall easily into place.

9. Your luck is scattered. Spiritually, you're high on the totem pole, so to speak, but it's difficult for you to focus your karma. Depending on the day, though, you can be equally lucky in love, career, family, and work.

Soul Number

Your soul number gives you an indication of how you look at things—your first instinctive reaction, before you begin to rationalize. It's important to know what your impulses are in order to be able to live with them.

The soul number comes from your given name, as it appears on your birth certificate. Let's go back to Winifred Alice Lee. When you convert each of the letters of her full name to a numerical value and add them all up, you should get 86. To reduce, add 8 and 6, which equal to 14; in turn, 1 + 4 = 5. The result is Winifred Alice Lee's soul number.

FACT

British philosopher and mathematician Bertrand Russell (1872–1970) stated, "Mathematics is, I believe, the chief source of the belief in eternal and exact truth, as well as in a super-sensible intelligible world" *(The History of Western Philosophy).*

Here are interpretations for each of the soul numbers:

1. At first glance, you're incredibly ambitious. You want to control, dominate, and to possess. That's okay, as long as you realize that you have to play by the rules and stay calm to get what you want. Don't obsess.

2. Stop trying to see everything from another person's point of view. It's time that you relied on your own thoughts and trusted your gut. On the other hand, if there is a companion in your life who has the same ideas you have, perhaps what you're doing is right. Think about it, and go on from there.

3. You take the side of the underdog before you hear both sides. This means you're easily influenced, and you can, at times, be a little naïve. Still, you are good at giving advice and are creative in your approach to things.

4. You're everyone's rock, but it's difficult to find someone that you can rely on and respect. Once you do find that person, you'll be functioning at 150 percent capacity. Get rid of people close to you who drain your energy. Your mission in life is not to be a saint, but to be happy.

5. You are more instinctive than analytical and prefer to find solutions quickly, without considering all sides. Unfortunately, you tend to make hasty decisions without listening to others. Take some time to get away from the problem before you make important decisions.

6. You feel responsible for making everyone else have a good time, which ruins your own enjoyment. Remember that a sunset can be just as beautiful when you watch it alone.

7. Try to feel things on a more emotional level. People don't want your sympathy, they want your empathy. If you feel more comfortable isolating yourself, pick someone to do that with, whether a lover or a friend. Having good company is more important than you realize.

8. Sometimes you see an easy solution to a problem but you don't recognize all the hard work needed to make it happen. You should try being more generous and more sensitive to others around you. Not everything has to do with your career.

9. You're good at figuring out right from wrong and your hunches are nearly always on the mark. Stop trying to guess what the other person is thinking and, instead, let them tell you. You'll learn something from the experience.

Identity Number

Your identity number describes how you are seen by the outside world, and how people interpret your appearance and behavior. You can calculate your identity by adding up the consonants in your name (whichever one you use every day). For example, for the name Julie

Miller, you add up the values of the consonants: J = 1, L = 3, M = 4, L = 3, L = 3, R = 9; 1 + 3 + 4 + 3 + 3 + 9 = 23; 2 + 3 = 5. This means that Julie's identity number is 5.

ALERT!

The letter "Y" can be used as either a consonant or a vowel. It is a vowel when it carries a vowel sound, as in "my" or "sky," and it's a consonant when it's attached to another vowel and doesn't carry its own vowel sound, as in "yes" or "beyond." Y is used as a vowel in the names Joey and Yvonne; it is a consonant in the names like Yaron and Meyer.

Here is what your identity number has to tell you:

1. People may see you as bossy or aggressive, though you may be as fierce as a de-clawed kitten. Try to be less opinionated or difficult, because these things affect your well-being. If you give in to others' demands, you may find that it causes you less stress.
2. People see you as a kind, persuasive individual. If this is an act, maybe it's time to make it real. If this is the way you are, are you using your influence for good? You have power over others. Use it wisely.
3. People may see you as an eclectic type or an individualist but you have the capacity for being traditional and practical-minded once in a while. It may be to your advantage to show people that, besides being socially adept and fun, you can also be grounded and stable. The key here is to give a more balanced, rounded-out appearance to others.
4. Others rely on you. They see you as dependable, solid, and a good decision-maker. If you'd prefer that they also see the more eccentric side of you, why not let it show? What are you waiting for? Sometimes a little craziness adds to the mystique. You don't always have to be predictable.
5. You're full of life, an attractive person who's got charm and sex appeal. But are they seeing the other side of you? You may sometimes feel inferior and strive to be something that you are not.

Be true to yourself and let all of your sides come through. People will only respect you for it.

6. People see you in one of two ways: either as a homebody and a martyr, or as a romantic idealist addicted to love. Either way, there needs to be more of a balance. If you're home all the time, let your wild side show a little. If you're always looking for love, try staying home once in a while.

7. You tend to be out of touch with things. People sometimes see you as a difficult person, though they would never tell you so. Some stay out of your way simply because they don't know how to communicate with you.

8. People either see you as too aggressive or too reticent. Neither one is good for your career. Evaluate your standing and make the changes that need to be made.

9. People see you as a generous and loyal friend. You may even have a great sexual allure to would-be love interests. The problem is, you go with your instinct and this may come across as intimidating. Try not to be too aggressive.

Spiritual Force Number

The spiritual force number has to do with something inside of you, an energy that needs to be released in order for you to realize your potential. To figure out your spiritual force number, you need to add up the letter values for each of the vowels in your name (again, this should be the name you use every day).

This time, let's take the name Ann Hanson as an example. There are three vowels in Ann's name: A = 1, A = 1, O = 6. Now, all you need to do is add up the digits: 1 + 1 + 6 = 8, which is Ann's spiritual force number.

Note that if Ann's name was only slightly different—if, for instance, it would have been Anne—her spiritual force number would have been completely different: A = 1, E = 5, A = 1, O = 6; 1 + 5 + 1 + 6 = 13; 1 + 3 = 4.

FACT

Albert Einstein once remarked, "If A is a success in life then A = X + Y + Z. Work is X, Y is play, and Z is keeping your mouth shut."

Here is what spiritual force numbers have to tell you:

1. You are a natural-born leader, though it may be a part of you that has been hidden thus far. The truth is, you are more than capable of managing a whole section of a company and of controlling your own destiny. Deal with your problems and go on to greatness.

2. You like being independent and a part of you feels weak for loving love in general. Eventually, this part of you is going to win out anyway. Forget what you've been taught. Sharing and relying on someone else is real strength, not vulnerability. You can love without losing who you are.

3. There's an energy inside you that might be blocked. If it's already surfaced, you've done the work that you needed to do. If it hasn't, why are you holding back? If you're working as an accountant but you'd love to be a painter, you need to figure out another way to combine your work and your passion. The real satisfaction will come when your soul and spirit are contented.

4. There's a strong, practical, reliable side of you that keeps trying to come out. Are you holding it back? Do you think it will make you boring or predictable? On the contrary, being strong and reliable are positive qualities. When you combine them with the rest of what makes you *you*, your life will head in the right direction.

5. You like to try new things and sometimes get easily bored by the mundane. You need to open yourself up to new experiences in order to feel like you're really alive. Forget about winning and revenge. Pride comes from knowing you're worth something, not by putting others down.

6. You know that romance and love guide your life too much, but you can't seem to do anything about it. You need to step back and prioritize. If you know that your career would improve if you let go of

some of your dependencies and love addictions, maybe it's something that you should work on. The problem is this: Do you care enough to change?

7. You're a private person and people respect you for that. Sometimes, though, it's nice to stop being so secretive and let people into your life.

8. You have it within you to be in an authoritative position at work. If you're always being ordered around, you're probably not happy. Let your natural good business sense shine.

9. Sometimes you know what other people are thinking. Don't analyze it. Stay true to yourself and others will respect you for it. Being overly sensitive will hinder you, not aid you.

Numbers for Everyday Life

You can also use numerology for everyday guidance. In love and in career, numbers appear in strange places. It's your job to find them and make them work for you. Your personal year number, too, will help you to understand how your luck, fortune, and general well-being are holding up in this period of your life.

Career Numbers

How can you use numerology at work? Well, here is one example. Let's say you set up an important work meeting or an interview on a specific day. Now, if you'd like to know what the general feeling of that day may be, simply add up the digits of the date to get a career number reading.

If the meeting is on March 2, 2004, add up $2 + 3 + 2 + 0 + 0 + 4 = 11$; $1 + 1 = 2$. Now, all you have to do is look up the interpretation, and you'll know whether this date is propitious for that meeting. Here are the interpretations for career numbers:

1. A good day to conquer your demons and set up camp. You're right there in the spotlight. Use finesse, and you've got them in the bag.

2. This is a good opportunity to iron out previous problems. If, however, you need a more powerful day for business, try dates linked with 1 or 8.

3. Today is the day you come up with a creative solution to a problem that has long haunted you as well as others. If people aren't responding to your alternative ways, however, lie low and give them time. It may just be that they're not ready to accept what they've been offered.

4. People will see you as their own personal messiah. You're balanced, grounded, and have a good hold on things today. Your career can benefit as a result. Make sure you add a little humor into your speech so it's not so dry and long-winded.

5. This is not the best day for work matters. Though they see you as capable and trustworthy, they may be looking for someone who has a stronger background, with more experience. Try to reschedule.

6. Responsibility is your middle name today. Unfortunately, people can see the ties you have to your family as a setback to your career. If this doesn't pose a problem to the situation, go ahead and schedule a meeting today.

7. Work matters bode well today but you may want to be more part of the group. Be social. Don't be so demanding and difficult.

8. This is your killer workday. Take advantage.

9. It can go both ways but, mostly, this is a good day for work matters. Your colleagues know how hard you've worked and they are supportive of you.

Numbers carry within them the potential for wisdom as well as for foolishness—for constructive as well as destructive behavior. Only you can choose which path you will take, and making the right choice requires wisdom.

Romantic Numbers

You can also use numerology to make plans for a romantic date or to decide when to take a vacation together. Again, add up the digits of a particular date (month, day, and year) to see if the time is right. Here is what the numbers mean.

1. You can steer things in the right direction without being so pushy. If you're stubborn by nature, put off a date that's linked with the number 1. If you simply want to make a partner understand how you feel, this is a good day to do so. Make sure, though, that you do it with tact.

2. You can't have a more perfect love day! This is a day when you can bend and blend in with the people around you. It's a good time to find middle ground with your partner.

3. It's a good day to be social. Your energy level is fully boosted. Let the others also see the stable part of you. Your seductive side is powerful on a day connected with the number 3.

4. If things are going really well already, this is a good day for love. If not, you may want to rethink the day. This day is good for making your partner feel secure and helping him or her with work problems. It is not, however, a day for spontaneity or frivolous fun. Think about it.

5. You're fiery, passionate, and proud today. You can sweep someone off his or her feet. Today is a day of fun and spontaneity.

6. This is a great love day. Make sure that the other person feels the same way. Don't be overly dramatic about things. Go into it with a clear head.

7. This is not a day for love. You're out of the loop and somewhat withdrawn. If you've always been the generous and giving one in the relationship, though, maybe today is a good day to let your other half pamper you.

8. Anything can happen on this day. If you want more security, pick a day linked with the number 3 or the number 6.

9. This is a nice, friendly day for love. Both parties are sensitive, playful, and giving.

Your Personal Year Number

In addition to checking specific dates, also consider your personal year number, which changes each time your birthday comes around. That's because you calculate your personal year number by adding up the digits of the date of your last birthday. So, for instance, if you were born on January 22, and your last birthday was on January 22, 2004, this is the date you need to use for your calculation: $1 + 2 + 2 + 2 + 0 + 0 + 4 = 11$; $1 + 1 = 2$.

In our example, the personal number for the year 2004 (as of January 22) is 2. Your personal year number affects how you relate to the world because it is the guiding force that will stay with you throughout the year, until the next birthday.

1. It's time for you to stop waiting on the sidelines for things to happen. This is your year to take action. For once, you can be a leader and not a follower. Be aggressive. People will take an interest in what you're doing only when they see that you are true to your convictions.
2. This year is a time when you need to work well with others. It also has to do with partnerships in love and with family. If you've been waiting to work on your social graces, now is the year to do so. Remember that what you give, you get back in return.
3. This year is a time to let loose and to let your creative side have a go at things. If your nature is somewhat bohemian, snap on those strange, artsy earrings—even if you're a lawyer. Small changes can create big (and positive) results. The "real you" is craving to come out. Let it.
4. This is the time to analyze what's gone wrong in the past, and make it count. You need to keep your feet on the ground and stop running off when things get too difficult. It may also be the time to make radical decisions in your life. If a relationship has become more of a chore than the fun it used to be, you need to either resolve your differences or cut it off. You're slowly drifting apart, anyway.
5. This is your year to travel and seek out adventures. You need to live life by your gut this year. Do something spontaneous. Instead of looking to please others, figure out what will make you happy and do it. Don't be so wrapped up in appearances.
6. This is the year to get ready for love. In other words, if you want to feel good about yourself, do everything you can to make it happen: work out, go on a diet, take some meditation classes, learn how to cook. This year is focused on you, family, romance, and love in general.
7. This may be a year when you need to conquer your demons, alone.

Seven is a number of independence and seclusion. If you've been meaning to write a book, hole yourself up in a room and do it.

8. Anything can happen this year. Eight is a wild card. Your strength lies in good business opportunities now. It's time to take a chance and change careers or even your address, if that's what your heart desires.

9. This is the year to reap the rewards of your efforts. You've been kind, generous, and a good friend. Trust your instincts and go with the flow. This will be a good year for you.

Numerology is common to all, but at the same time it can be very personal. Numbers are living energies, and they are everywhere, even as a part of you. That means that you have within you an exact understanding of what they are.

Chapter 12

Astrology: Secrets of the Sun Signs

This chapter is meant to give you a good introduction to the fascinating field of astrology. For now, you should rely on the help of a professional astrologer to create a birth chart for you and watch the stars and their behavior in relation to your sign. However, if you'd like to delve deeper into astrology and create your own birth chart, *The Everything® Astrology Book* is an excellent guide to how astrology works and how you can use it in your life.

Astrology 101

Everyone knows about astrology. Horoscopes are published in newspapers and magazines, and the question "What's your sign?" is pretty common. But astrology is so much more than an affectation or an easy parlor trick. It's a method that has been studied for millennia and is widely used as a gateway in divination.

Astrology is based on the belief that the movements of stars and other celestial bodies affect our lives and the events that occur on Earth. Astrologers study the placement, movement, and relationships between celestial bodies to predict the future based on each person's astrological signs (or, more specifically, sun sign) as well as the other aspects in her own personal chart.

Astrology can't provide us with "day to day" predictions, but it can alert you to gateways of opportunity that you can take advantage of. As the stars move through your birth chart, there will be times that are most appropriate for certain undertakings and less appropriate for others, and that's where astrology can help you. If you go beyond your horoscope and analyze your entire chart, you can better understand what is happening in the universe and how it relates to you at a specific period in time. Of course, what you do with these opportunities is up to you.

QUESTION?

Can astrology predict what's going to happen in the future?
Yes and no. Astrology can give you an idea of what can happen at a particular point in time—it gives you an open door, which you can either enter or walk past.

How It Came About

Stargazing and the fascination with the heavens have existed since the creation of mankind. It is said that the ancient Babylonians brought astrology to Greece in the fourth century B.C. After that, it spread through Europe and was heavily practiced in Italy before the arrival of the

Christian era. Other believers in astrology were the Egyptians, the Hindus, the ancient Chinese, and the Etruscans.

Somewhere around the late Middle Ages, astrology became a more complex art. For a complete birth chart (also called natal chart or horoscope), you need to know the exact time of your birth, down to the hour, as well as where exactly you came into this world—that is, the location of the city or town. Based on this information, the astrologer looks at the positions of the moon, the constellations, and the sun and its planets during the time of your birth. What the astrologer sees is then translated into personality and character strengths and weaknesses that you are likely to possess. In the framework of astrology, the planets (including the sun and the moon) influence the way we act, think, and feel.

FACT

In Europe, between the fourteenth and fifteenth century, no self-respecting monarch would make a decision or proclamation without first consulting the court astrologer. These astrologers were the royal guides or counselors of the kingdom.

The Twelve Houses

If you think of the sky as a circle and you divide it into twelve parts, each part is known as a house. As the sun moves around the sky over the course of the year, it travels from one house to the next, until it makes a circle. Your sun sign is the house where the sun appeared on the day of your birth in relation to your birth's location, and it is the most important part of your astrological chart. (If you don't know your sun sign, check **TABLE 12-1**.)

Because it's difficult to section off the universe into precise parts, some gray areas still remain when it comes to determining a person's sun sign. Therefore, people who are born "on the cusp"—at the edge of a house— may possess traits from more than one sign. For example, if you are born on February 18 or February 19, read the sections on both Aquarius and Pisces and see for yourself which one may best describe you.

◀ Sun signs.

TABLE 12-1 TWELVE SUN SIGNS

Sun Sign	Date of Your Birth	Sun Sign	Date of Your Birth
Aries (ram)	March 21–April 19	Libra (scales)	Sept 23–Oct 23
Taurus (bull)	April 20–May 20	Scorpio (scorpion)	Oct 24–Nov 21
Gemini (twins)	May 21–June 21	Sagittarius (archer)	Nov 22–Dec 21
Cancer (crab)	June 22–July 22	Capricorn (sea goat)	Dec 22–Jan 19
Leo (lion)	July 23–August 22	Aquarius (water bearer)	Jan 20–Feb 18
Virgo (virgin)	August 23–Sept 22	Pisces (fish)	Feb 19–March 20

In addition to your sun sign, other important information that goes into your birth chart is your ascendant (your rising sign) and your moon sign. Basically, your sun sign is your natural essence, the way you are; your ascendant is the way you see life; and your moon is linked with your emotions—how you feel and how you deal with problems that arise.

Your Sun Sign: Aries to Pisces

This section contains the description of each sun sign. Again, if you're interested in getting a full birth chart, you should consult with a professional astrologer. Horoscopes should be done correctly, and there are a lot of nuances to keep in mind.

Aries (Ram)

The 365-day zodiacal year begins on March 21 with Aries. Therefore, Aries represents the "child" stage in life, perhaps from birth to seven or eight years of age. Aries people are sometimes like children, naturally curious and inquisitive. They also tend to be a little self-centered and may get irrationally frustrated when they don't get their way. Many Aries have a quick temper as well.

Aries people are ruled by the planet Mars. They are born leaders and see the world as something they can conquer, if they decide to put their minds to it. In business, they're aggressive and dominant in their dealings with others (though they always have enough flirtatious charm and personality to spare).

Aries people are also very physical beings and are likely to be interested in many different types of sports. Less evolved Aries could be labeled "unfeeling" because they normally don't let emotions rule them in any way. Though family may be very important to them, they may have difficulty being faithful to one partner and, possibly, with sticking it out and working through problems that may arise in a marriage. They can also be idealistic and very creative individuals.

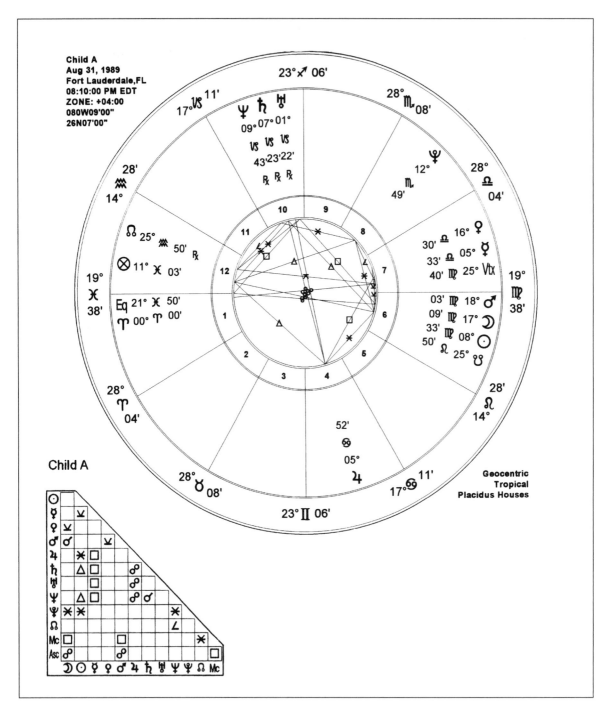

▲ A sample birth chart.

Taurus (Bull)

Taurus is the second sign of the zodiac and is ruled by Venus. This house represents the next stage after birth in a child's life, from approximately eight to fourteen or fifteen years of age. This is the time when a child learns about discipline and knowing right from wrong, and finds her place in the world.

Taurus people can be quite stubborn and headstrong. They like to be in charge to be more in control of the outcome. Taurus individuals are also very interested in human nature. They love to watch and analyze things happening around them. They use what they learn to determine "truths" about people, places, and events. They also like to plan things out, and normally go about doing this in a methodical fashion, albeit with drawn-out meticulousness.

Like children discovering the limitations of their ability in the world, they are also very physical individuals and can be tempted by (and excel in) all physical activities that stimulate their senses—eating, sex, and general exercise and sports. In this way, they can be very sensual individuals.

It is said that many Taurus people also possess certain physical characteristics. Astrologers say that it's easy to single out a Taurus person by his or her stocky build and/or strong, solid frame.

Gemini (Twins)

Gemini is the third sign of the zodiac, and is ruled by Mercury. In terms of the universal life stages, Gemini is a stage of teen years, from the age of fourteen to about twenty-one. Neither a child nor a grownup, the Gemini individual is still learning his place in the world.

Gemini people like to rely on intellect and communication skills in order to get their way. They're born storytellers and can exaggerate, create, and manipulate an account so much so that it may begin sounding more like a fairy tale than the truth. In fact, they can get so wrapped up in a story that they later have trouble distinguishing between what was fact and what was fiction.

By nature, Gemini people can be quite capricious, changing their minds and their ideas from minute to minute. But at their best, Gemini individuals are interesting, funny, charming, outspoken, and sociable. They seek adventures and get a thrill out of creating problems and drama. Gemini people are also able to rationalize things away, and may seem unemotional or unsympathetic.

Cancer (Crab)

Cancer is the fourth sign of the zodiac, ruled by the moon. Cancer people are considered to be at the stage in life that can be likened to a young adult in their early to late twenties. They know what needs to be done and like to do it with more finesse and less aggressive action than that of their sun sign predecessors (Aries, Taurus, and Gemini).

Cancers are often ruled by emotions; they tend to be moody and quite sensitive. Cancers are good friends to have because they can be sympathetic to the needs of others. But they may expect their friends to understand where they're coming from at all times, though they may change that specific mind frame in an instant. If they choose to be, Cancers can also be very persuasive and even manipulative. And less evolved Cancers can be downright sneaky. However, Cancers can be domestic, family-loving homebodies and many times prefer a nice glass of wine and dinner at home to running around town.

Leo (Lion)

Leo is the fifth sign of the zodiac, and it is ruled by the sun. Leo's universal stage of life is comparable to a young adult in their late twenties to early thirties. Like all people in this phase of life, Leos want to show the world that they've "arrived." Leos tend to be showy and like to do all things in a big way.

Leos can be proud to the point of being stubborn, but there is nothing they won't do for a true friend. Loyal in their own way, they will defend any person or cause they see as being important and will always take the side of the underdog. They can be affectionate, playful, genuine, and many times have "sunny" personalities. Though they seem to be very social creatures, they can become withdrawn and altogether antisocial if none of the attention is focused on them. Leos adore praise. They forgive easily, but never forget.

Many Leos are drawn toward creative professions, choosing to work behind the scenes or on center stage. In general, they like to control things but manage to do it in a quiet manner (with tact and taste). Rich or poor, all Leos love to spend money and dislike having to hold back when they get the urge to spend. Consequently, they also don't understand, and frequently despise, stinginess in others.

FACT

Psychiatrist Carl Gustav Jung studied many methods of divination and their connection to the human psyche. His studies in astrology included a comparison of married couples, utilizing the two individuals' sun signs, ascendants, and moons.

Virgo (Virgin)

Virgo is the sixth sign of the zodiac; like Geminis, Virgos are ruled by the planet Mercury. Think of Virgos as those who have reached real adulthood, in their mid-thirties to early forties. Like people at this stage in life, Virgos act as if they have some experience behind them and know how to handle themselves in a practical, methodical way. In fact, sometimes they can be too strict and not flexible enough in their ways.

Virgo people are orderly. They are serious individuals who also know how to have a good time. But they are more concerned with the big picture than with moment-to-moment acquisitions. Therefore, all Virgos have a plan and try not to stray off the path they've constructed for themselves until their goals are realized. Virgos tend to be very bright; they're always aware of what's going on around them.

Many Virgos like to be part of a small group (of family or friends) and are usually not found wandering and traveling around the world on a whim (like Aries or Gemini). They're hard workers and can sometimes be perfectionists. Always striving for the best in everything, in fact, Virgos can be exceptionally picky when choosing close friends or a mate.

Libra (Scales)

Libra is the seventh sign of the zodiac and is ruled by Venus. If you were to place Libra in a stage of universal life, it would be in the early to late forties. Like a seasoned adult at this stage of the game, a Libra takes her time in doing things, weighing the odds and watching how the scales lean. For this reason, Libras may sometimes seem indecisive but, in truth, they simply prefer to do things without pressure or influence from others. For the Libras, beauty, harmony, and peace are life's necessities. When searching for a home, a place of work, or even a mate, Libras are often won over by sheer comeliness.

Libras are fair, diplomatic individuals and expect the same from others. Less evolved Libras may be dissatisfied with life in general and are prone to self-pity. Some Libras may even cause problems around them and then sit back and watch the situation develop. Libras can be very expressive (sensually or with words); many have a highly developed sense of humor. They can also be quite charming and attractive.

Scorpio (Scorpion)

Scorpio is the eighth sign of the zodiac and is ruled by Pluto. In the universal life stages, a Scorpio is in the early to middle fifties. Like most people at this age, Scorpios have learned to understand human nature quite a bit.

Scorpios can get what they want by being crafty—they know that the best way to attack is from behind. They're incredibly secretive, in a practical sort of way; you may hear a Scorpio say, "Why does anyone have to know my business? They don't need to know my business." Many Scorpios have a dark, elusive quality to them and they're very sensual individuals. They can be quite passionate and yet cynical at the same time. Even the more easygoing Scorpios always have a certain kind of nervous energy waiting to be released.

There is a danger of less evolved Scorpios falling into a rut or depression, and they need to be wary of using antidepressants as a crutch. Scorpios can be self-mocking and have a slightly sarcastic edge to their sense of humor. They're jealous and possessive, even to the point of obsession. If they've been hurt, they can be quite vengeful. If they're in love, they can be charming, sexy, and very generous.

We discussed before how all methods of divination are linked in some way. Many Tarot cards represent certain signs of astrology. The card that symbolizes Virgo is The Hermit; Scorpios are strongly connected to the Death card. Libras are related to the Empress card and the Justice card.

Sagittarius (the Archer)

Sagittarius is the ninth sign of the zodiac and is influenced by Jupiter. The universal stage of life for Sagittarius is equivalent to late fifties and early sixties. Like someone at this age, Sagittarians feel comfortable with their place in the world and don't hesitate to move around from port to port.

Though Sagittarians are notorious adventure-seekers, they can be faithful, true companions when they decide to finally settle down. They're the first to tell you what they think and they never hold back the truth. In fact, they're so determined to say what's on their minds that they frequently lack the tact they need to preserve the peace, and may appear a bit harsh.

Ignorance easily annoys Sagittarians. For a Sagittarius, there is only one right way to do something. They don't waste their time trying to show others the right way. Instead, they're off doing something they consider to be more worthwhile. Their interests are broad and many. They love sports that give them a feeling of freedom, like skiing and sailing. They also love exotic food, cultures, languages, and so on. In one moment, they can swing from being incredibly modest to seriously cocky.

Capricorn (the Goat)

Capricorn is the tenth sign of the zodiac and is ruled by the planet Saturn. If you had to place Capricorn into the universal stages of life, you would have a person in their mid- to late sixties. Like someone at this age, Capricorn longs for stability, comfort, and security in the form of personal relationships as well as in material wealth.

Capricorns are instinctively great teachers and love to be sought out for their knowledge. In fact, many Capricorns understand even the most tedious tidbits of all things related to science or mathematics; they're like sponges, soaking up the information so that they may use it at a later date. Capricorns are either skeptics or idealists. The skeptics think that when things work out, it was just dumb luck. The idealists, on the other hand, believe that everything is meant to go well for them, and their approach to life can be somewhat childlike, in wonder and awe of everything around them.

All Capricorns, though, have somewhat of a mean streak. If they feel they're being tested, they'll lash out. They can be critical of others and they never forget a word or deed that's been said or done to them. Even ten years later, they are capable of using someone's words from the past against them.

Capricorns can also be very loving, faithful family partners and, when they feel they've met the one for them, will express their love sincerely. The only reason many Capricorns marry later in life than most is because they feel they need financial stability and security before starting a family. Less evolved Capricorns tend to be opportunistic, sticking close to people who can help them in financial matters or with their career. Though some Capricorns can be seen as "cold" or "apathetic" individuals, it's mostly because they don't like to share their suffering with others, mainly preferring to deal with hard times alone, without (false) sympathy.

ALERT!

Though they're considered to be a fire sign, most Sagittarians have an earthy, serious quality to them, though they love making others laugh. Respect for their ideas and their authority is very important to Sagittarius people.

Aquarius (Water Bearer)

Aquarius is the eleventh sign of the zodiac, ruled by Uranus. The period in life that Aquarius can most be likened to is that of a person in their seventies, someone who has seen it all and chooses to live life to the beat of a different drum.

In fact, all Aquarians are unique and eclectic in their tastes in general. They're mostly unconventional and are curious about human nature—about what makes people tick. They're also very intuitive. Aquarian people are frequently patient and interesting individuals who have friends from different corners of society. Aquarians are, generally, the least judgmental of all the signs. Mostly, they admire someone for being who they are.

Aquarians like to get their way but will never force an issue. Even if they have many setbacks in life, they always seem to land on their feet. And others seem to be drawn to them for their confidence and easy manner. The only drawback of this is that people with many problems seek out Aquarians for help and for friendship. Therefore, Aquarians always seem to have a group of fans and followers whose issues threaten to weigh them down.

Pisces (Fish)

Pisces is the twelfth sign of the zodiac, ruled by the planet Neptune. In the phases of universal life, Pisces may fit in the category of a senior adult, someone in their late seventies and early eighties. Even at a young age, Pisces are said to have "old souls" and are more mature than others of the same age.

Many Pisces are quite refined and may sometimes be labeled as snobs, but talking with them will lead you to throw away the characterization, because they are personable and friendly (even if they don't like you). Pisces women are their partner's rock, meaning that the one who's with them feels he has won a prize after he has won her over—she's selective, secure, and knows what she wants. And she's good to her partner, too. A Pisces woman isn't likely to stay with someone unless she's convinced that he will devote his entire life to trying to please her. Pisces women like what they consider to be strong men.

Pisces men, on the other hand, are somewhat misguided in this respect. Many times they tend to focus their energy on women who are not worth their time and/or effort. Pisces men are generally weaker than Pisces women. The Pisces men have an idea of what their "perfect" woman may be and, as a result, can be quite dreamy, possibly to the point of being depressed over a woman who may not even be good for them. Their dark side may lead them through a few obsessions but, when they finally find the right partner, they can be generous, romantic, and downright poetic. Both Pisces women and men are sensitive and good listeners.

FACT

Interestingly enough, astrology gave birth to various everyday English words. According to experts, words such as consider, disaster, conjunction, and influenza (the flu) all have origins linked with astrology.

Four Basic Elements

The ancients believed that life is made up of four essential and basic elements—fire, air, water, and earth—and they have divided the sun signs accordingly:

- **Fire signs:** Sagittarius, Leo, and Aries.
- **Air signs:** Libra, Aquarius, and Gemini.
- **Earth signs:** Taurus, Capricorn, and Virgo.
- **Water signs:** Pisces, Cancer, and Scorpio.

Note that Aquarius is not a water sign. Though it does represent the water bearer, it is actually an air sign.

Element Compatibility

If it's friendship you seek or love from a partner, a sun sign will hardly be enough of an indication as to whether or not the union will be a positive one. Some of the best couples around are Sagittarius and Pisces (fire and water), or Aries and Virgo (air and earth). Though, theoretically, these love matches shouldn't work by virtue of their utter opposed outlooks on things, they sometimes just do. Perhaps it's thanks to that old saying that opposites attract; more likely, you'll have to delve deeper into both individuals' charts to find, in fact, that there are other corresponding signs throughout them that help make the partnership thrive.

How does this work? Let's say that your chart is replete with the elements air and water. Your boyfriend's birth chart, instead, is mostly earth. For all intents and purposes, this love arrangement shouldn't work, right? Not necessarily. For instance, the only earth element you have in your chart is in Mercury. Although this may not seem as important as having a compatible sun or moon sign, Mercury is the way in which you communicate. And good communication, we all know, is one of the keys to success in a healthy relationship. Don't discount a new lover or friend based solely on their sun sign or ascendant. You may miss out on a great opportunity to create more happiness for your future.

Chapter 13

Divining Dreams

Throughout history, we have wondered about the meaning of our dreams. In many ancient cultures, dreams were thought to have prophetic meaning. Others thought that you could control "real life" events through your dreams. Sigmund Freud, who developed psychoanalysis, suggested that dreams are simply a means through which your unconscious thoughts manifest themselves. What are dreams? And can they really tell you something about your future? This chapter will help you find out.

The Question of Interpretation

What do our dreams mean? Where do they come from? What can we learn from them? Are there regular as well as prophetic dreams? Or are all dreams prophetic? And why are many dreams so bizarre? Why do we dream about losing our teeth, or about being naked in public? Is there something to it? Is it a prediction of some kind, or is there some other higher meaning?

You could buy a dream book and look up each symbol. For example, your dream has a bird in it. What does it mean? Well, you look up "bird" and it says "a fortunate sign. Good news is coming." And while this may be helpful, it can also sometimes be frustrating. What if the bird in your dream turned into your mother? Or what if it was talking to you? Or what if it was impersonating Mick Jagger? It seems that these radically different dreams can't possibly have one interpretation.

FACT

Psychiatrist Carl Gustav Jung said, "In the last analysis, most of our difficulties come from losing contact with our instincts, with the age-old unforgotten wisdom stored up in us. And where do we make contact with this old man in us? In our dreams" (*Psychological Reflections*).

So What Are We to Do?

The key to dream interpretation lies in psychology. Don't worry—you don't have to have a doctorate in the subject. What you do need is to be able to use your instinct and your common sense. Dreams are almost never literal. In a dream, you may have special powers—crossing from one dimension to another, defeating fire-breathing dragons, climbing the Himalayas, seeing yourself from the outside looking in, and nearly dying ten times the same night all in pursuit of something unbeknownst to you.

Ultimately, dreams are about soul-searching. You can ignore things that happen in your everyday life, but during your sleep your fears, desires, and even psychic visions come to pay a friendly visit (or scare the bejeebies out of you)—and you don't have a whole lot of control over it.

By examining your dreams, piece by piece, deciphering and decoding them, you can accomplish one monumental task—directing your destiny. By understanding your dreams, you can better understand yourself and gain the knowledge and the confidence to find a better, more spiritual (and healthy) path to greatness.

This chapter will examine four categories of dreams—everyday (normal) dreams, fear or anxiety dreams, dreams of desire, and prophecy dreams—as well as how to interpret them.

Everyday Dreams

Everyday dreams are normal dreams—but what's "normal" anyway? Certainly not the dream you had about your mailman. When you're awake, you rarely think of this guy, and then all of a sudden he's at the center of your dream world, fighting and defeating the three-eyed brain-sucking trolls that are after you—and conquering your heart as well!

This is what we call a "test" dream. It's an everyday dream, because it's simply you, your unconscious, testing out the things you would never even consider doing in real life. Does this mean you should go out on a date with your mailman? No—unless you really want to. The point is, this dream has no higher meaning. It's simply letting you test out possibilities.

Here are other examples of everyday dreams:

- You watch a movie with vampires in it and then you have a dream in which you're knocking around and killing some vampires. (Another version: You and your friend turn into vampires.)
- You meet someone who reminds you of an acquaintance you haven't thought about in years, and then you have a dream about that old acquaintance.
- You're on a diet, trying to lose weight, and you have a dream about food.
- You've been thinking about going on vacation and later dream about surfing in Hawaii or hiding out from the KGB in communist Russia.

- Someone is getting on your nerves at work and you have a dream that you're a gladiator in the Coliseum in ancient Rome—and your colleague is your opponent!

Everyday dreams may have symbols, but you have to look at the overall general theme of the dream to determine what it is your unconscious is trying to sort out. Chances are, if the dream is based on everyday happenings—even if it takes on a surreal, unnatural setting—you can rest assured that you're not receiving word passed down by the heavens.

Fear or Anxiety Dreams

Dreams that elicit fear and anxiety are fairly common. Fear dreams can run the gamut from the Mafia don with a pistol chasing you down a dark alley, to your baby brother becoming a giant and stepping on you, to your teeth falling out. Most of the time, these fears are irrational and don't pose a real threat in real life. What are the chances of your brother becoming a giant? But that's of no consequence—it's terrifying nevertheless. A fear or anxiety dream is actually a test dream taken to the next level.

These dreams usually relate to fears or issues you've pushed aside or tried to ignore. Monsters and supernatural dangers in fear and anxiety dreams are often symbolic of real-life fears. Or it may be your way of testing how much you could handle. What on earth would you do if demons really wandered around in your backyard? Your dream can show you how you would react.

For example, you know that the chances of your getting into an elevator and having it bounce out of the building, skyrocket to the heavens, and then drop five thousand stories with you in it, is not something that's about to happen any time soon. Yet, it's perfectly possible that you may have a dream about it. That's strange, you think. I'm not even scared of heights and I certainly have no fear of elevators.

What is your unconscious trying to tell you? Perhaps in this dream you are trying to deal with your fear of losing control. Don't try to take this dream apart and look for "elevator" in a dream dictionary. The symbolism is in the entire dream, not what each symbol means in itself. An "out of control" dream has to do with the fear you have of something happening in your life that you can't get a grip on.

Dreaming of being chased is an indication that your life (according to your unconscious) is not up to par and it's coming back around to get you. It doesn't matter who is after you, whether it's your mother-in-law or hairy orange monsters. Study the characters in your dream to determine what it is you're really running away from, then get to work on resolving your issues.

Other classic fear/anxiety dreams include standing on stage in front of a hundred people and not being able to remember your lines, or standing in the middle of a public square, naked, with everyone gawking at you. Incidentally, the "naked" dream can also be a desire dream, depending on how you perceive your nakedness in the dream. If people have a positive reaction to you, for example, and you also enjoy and/or revel in your exhibitionism in the dream, it means that your wish is to expose yourself, to make yourself vulnerable to others. This is a good sign, and a healthy one.

Dreams of Desire

It's easy to confuse desire dreams with prophecy dreams. Dreams of desire involve wish fulfillment (or wish negation). In other words, your unconscious creates a scene in which you get what you want and live happily ever after (or you get the opposite of what you want and you don't live happily ever after).

If, for example, you have a dream that your significant other is cheating on you, does it mean that it's really true? Or that it's going to happen? Probably not, because this is another "what if" dream—you are testing the limits of reality. If you are single and have a dream of meeting your perfect mate and bringing her home to meet your family, is it really going to happen? Is this a prophecy dream? Probably not. Again, this is a wish dream. Keep in mind that wish/desire dreams can be positive or negative.

ALERT!

All dreams (except prophecy dreams) are your unconscious mind's way of exploring "what if" scenarios. If you're against hunting as a sport, and you dream of doing it, it doesn't mean that you secretly wish you could go hunting.

Here are additional examples of desire dreams:

- Your friend takes the only lifeboat and leaves you stranded on a deserted island.
- You're at a big premiere with Sylvester Stallone and everyone's taking your picture.
- You're in a bathing suit at a beach party and everyone is complimenting you on what a great body you have.
- Your friends are talking about you and you're invisible to them, listening to what they're saying.
- In real life, you're against the killing of animals and hunting, in general. In your dream, you're wearing fur or are out hunting.

Prophecy Dreams

Now we're into difficult territory. Prophecy dreams sometimes have a mix of all the other dream categories, so they're hard to pinpoint. Usually, though, if you've had a prophecy dream, you know it. If you're not sure, you probably didn't have one. Prophecy dreams involve advice from a strange or unknown source; seeing a situation before it happens; and strong symbolism, which you can somehow interpret.

Advice from a Strange or Unknown Source

Let's say you have a dream in which your dog talks to you and gives you advice. This can be an everyday dream or a prophecy dream. How can you tell the difference? Well, if the source of this knowledge comes from you, from your unconscious, it's an everyday dream: You're using the dog in your dream as a way for you to talk to yourself. But, on the other hand, if you have no idea where the things your dog says came from, chances are you're receiving a gift, words coming from a higher spiritual level.

Here's another example: In your dream, a woman walks up to you in the street and tells you that if you don't stop eating hamburgers, you're going to have health problems and pass out in a Laundromat. Is this a prophecy dream? No, this is your unconscious warning you of things you're already probably well aware of but, perhaps, have chosen to ignore.

> While we're dreaming, we're also solving the little or big problems in our lives. Because we don't have the time (or the will) to handle everything at once, we push back things we don't want to deal with at the moment and they filter into our dreams as a result.

On the other hand, let's say that you have a dream about a queen who tells you to take her hand, and you have no idea what it means, either in the dream or in waking life. This is probably prophetic advice. At some point in the near future, you'll be in a situation in which you'll have to use this information. It's up to you to figure out when. It could happen when you're in a meeting at work or when you're strolling down the street with your significant other. In any case, you'll actually feel the two realities come together. The moment will have a kind of slow-motion effect and you'll sense that this is where your dream world meets the real world. That's how you'll know.

Seeing a Situation Before It Happens

This kind of dream is rare. Many times, what seems like a dream that will come true in reality is actually a testing dream. Plus, there is a problem with assuming that a testing dream is a prophecy dream—ever heard of the concept of self-fulfilling prophecy? If you believe something will happen, you will start a chain of events that will actually lead to it happening.

So, for example, if you have a dream in which you and your sister have a big fight and then she storms out the house, angry, and has a car accident, what does this mean? Does it mean that she's going to have a car accident? Should you be extra nice to her so that you two don't quarrel? Well, yes, be nice to her, by all means. You can even warn her to drive safely, as well. But chances are, this is not a prophecy dream. It's an everyday dream that tests your fears. Most prophecy dreams involve more symbolism. When you have one, you will know it for sure.

Strong Symbolism

When it comes to dreams, symbols cannot be translated into a universal language. This is because your unconscious is doing the interpreting. Each one of us is a separate, unique entity with different built-in features and filters that affect how we see the world. Therefore, even if a higher force is passing on a prophetic message to you, your dream will simply give you a picture in accordance with that which your unconscious finds comfortable or familiar. And this is what makes the dream easier for you to digest, absorb, and understand. So, while a dream book of universal signs may be helpful, the symbols in your dream will not necessarily mean the same thing that they do for others.

FACT

Dream divination differs from the I Ching, the Tarot, runes, tealeaf readings, astrology, and so forth. In dreams, the universal energy goes straight through you (not through a prop), which is why you must always translate the symbols according to what they mean to you.

Here is an example: One woman has a prophetic dream that only occurs when a member of her family is about to pass over. Instead of the family member coming into her dream to visit her (a common happening in prophecy dreams of this sort), she dreams of water. And while this may seem strange to most people, this woman knows that when she has this kind of "water" dream, it is an indication that someone she knows is about to pass away.

Water, as a universal symbol, usually means prosperity, happiness, and rebirth, so it's odd that this woman would dream of water when the theme of her prophecy dream deals with a relative passing away. The point is, each person's symbolism is different, and you should construct your own dream glossary. This is essential in order to interpret prophecy dreams.

Remembering Dreams

If you want to get the most out of your dreams, the first step is to remember them. The best way to remember your dreams is to write them down as soon as you wake up. Otherwise, it will be almost impossible for you to recall the details even a few hours later. When you are no longer in your dream state, your conscious mind tries to find logic in the series of happenings which occur (or have occurred) in your dream. In other words, it tries to make sense of something that may not have very much sense or order to it. Then, when it fails to do so, you automatically forget the dream.

Keeping a dream journal will help you to remember your dreams, but it has other benefits as well. For instance, it will allow you to keep track of how your dreams change, and you may notice patterns that you would have otherwise missed.

Keeping a Dream Journal

Here's what to include in your daily dream journal:

- **Dream descriptions:** Write down everything you can remember the moment you wake up. To remind yourself, keep the journal and a pen next to your bed.
- **Symbols:** Keep track of your personal dream symbols, especially those that occur periodically.

- **Feelings:** How did you feel in the dream? Writing down your feelings may help you make sense of the dream—a lot of the time the feelings are more important than the dream's plot.
- **Characters:** Are the people in your dream from your present or past—or are they strangers? If you're always dreaming of people from your distant past, for example, chances are that your unconscious is still trying to figure out events from your childhood.
- **Dream category:** Categorize each of your dreams. Was it an everyday dream, a fear/anxiety dream, a desire/wish dream, or a prophecy dream? By writing it down, you'll start noticing a pattern that will help you become more aware of your unconscious and how it is assimilating your thoughts right now. (E)

Chapter 14

The Truth in Tealeaves

Divination by reading tealeaves is known as tasseography or tasseomancy. Many people have heard of gypsies using tealeaves in divination, but did you know that it is actually an ancient divination tool originally practiced by the Chinese? To find out how you can read the future in tealeaves for yourself and for others, all you need is this book, some tea, a teacup, and questions about your future!

The Practice of Reading Tealeaves

Nearly everyone has tea stashed somewhere in the cupboard—and that's pretty much all you need to conduct a tealeaf reading, plus boiling water, a cup and saucer, some very general knowledge, and good intentions. You don't even need a strainer. It can be done in the privacy of your own home with a minimum of fuss and hardly any expense. Just brew a cup of tea, pour it, and you're set.

In some cultures, fortunetellers prefer using coffee grounds (especially grounds of Turkish coffee) rather than tealeaves. In fact, coffee is a reasonable alternative. If you decide to use coffee grounds, simply follow the same steps as you would for tealeaf readings.

As with astrology, I Ching, runes, and Tarot cards, your intuition and an open mind will help you with tasseography. Remember: No method of divination is an exact science—everything is open to interpretation. For instance, seeing the shape of a circle anywhere in your teacup is generally a positive sign. It can mean completion of a project, trust, good fortune, and good news. If you're reading for a friend and her question has something to do with a love relationship, a complete circle may confirm or foretell an up-and-coming marriage proposal. When you get the feel of it, you, too, will find and create new shapes and meanings that make sense for you. There is no right and wrong—only what's right for you.

A Little History

Reading tealeaves has been around for as long as people have been drinking tea, which is about 5,000 years. Though the practice originated in China, where people first cultivated and drank tea, the modern version of tasseography may have its origins in ancient Greece, where people practiced the art of reading dregs (wine residue) after drinking wine.

Tea didn't find its way to Europe until the seventeenth century, and even then it was a luxury item used mostly for medicinal purposes. Tealeaf reading didn't catch on until the eighteenth and nineteenth centuries, when drinking tea and coffee became more common. Since then, like all other forms of divining the future, tealeaf reading has continued to evolve into what it is today.

FACT

The concept of teatime came about in a very interesting manner. Legend has it that the idea became all the rage thanks to King Charles II (1630–1685), a British monarch, who made it a practice to drink tea throughout the day.

Brew, Serve, and See!

Now, why don't we get started? Before you begin, you may want to place some candles around, dim the lights, and put on some appropriate music (for a review of how to set the right mood, see Chapter 5). Remember to center yourself and to clear all thoughts from your mind.

What You'll Need

Get a midsized cup (preferably wider around the top) with a handle. Always use white, without patterns, to make sure you can see the images clearly. You will also need a saucer that matches the cup (again, white is preferable). To brew tea, you will need a teapot or another container for boiling water. Good tea for divination must be loose-leaf. (Using a tea bag won't work!) Tea such as Chinese and Indian mixtures as well as orange pekoe and Earl Grey are good because the leaves aren't too big and are much easier to read. And if the tea tastes good, that's definitely a plus.

Brewing Tea

Use cold water to fill your teapot and bring the water to a boil. Place the loose tea in the pot—use as much of it as you like. Leaving the pot on the stove, turn off the heat, place a cover on top, and let it sit for about five minutes. Now you're ready. Forget the strainer. The point is to get the tea leaves into the cup. And don't worry—there is absolutely nothing wrong with taking a spoon and scooping out extra tealeaves if your pour didn't catch enough. If your focus is on the task at hand, don't let superstition ruin your fun. Once the cup is filled, let it cool down a bit and let the tealeaves float down to the bottom.

ALERT!

Always use cold water when you're preparing the tea. Psychics who rely on tasseography believe that cold water makes a better cup because it contains more oxygen and is generally more pure than hot water.

Tea Time

The person whose future will be read should be the one to drink the tea, so if you are reading for yourself, enjoy it! As you drink, take your time and concentrate on a specific question. If your thoughts are jumbled, your answer will be, too. Try not to talk during your focus time. Block out everything while you sip. Relax and enjoy the moment. And be careful not to swallow the tealeaves. When you have only a drop of liquid left in the cup, it's time to begin.

Hold the cup by the handle in your left hand if you're right-handed (or vice versa). Think again about your question or wish and say it out loud. Swirl the teacup in a clockwise motion three times or as many times as it takes for you to feel good about the timing. Note: If you are reading for someone else, let that person swirl the cup and ask the question herself.

Carefully and quickly turn the teacup upside down into the saucer. This will drain the excess liquid and help scatter the tealeaves around the cup. Count to seven or any number that's lucky for you, and turn the teacup back over. There should be no drops of moisture left in the cup, only clumps of tealeaves. When the teacup is right side up, make sure that the handle is facing the reader, because the handle is the point of reference to which everything comes back. The handle and the zone around it represent your home life and family, as well as people you know and people you're about to meet.

A Spot of Tea

The first moment you glance into the teacup, one particular shape should attract your attention. What is it? Whatever image first strikes you is what you should stick with, even if it makes no sense. If you see Mickey Mouse and don't find it listed in the symbol index, don't ignore it! Think about how it could possibly relate back to the divination question. Could it be that the querent has unresolved childhood issues? Maybe it has something to do with her children? It sounds far-fetched, but you'd be surprised what springs to a person's mind and how accurate the figures construed by the reader sometimes are.

One psychic reader did a reading for a woman and saw a fire-breathing dragon in the tealeaves. The woman's question was about her boy, eight years old, who seemed completely uninterested in his school studies, to the point of being detached from life and the people around him. It turned out that the boy's problems stemmed from a fixation on video games—including one featuring a fire-breathing dragon.

QUESTION?

Does it matter how many times I swirl the cup and in which direction I do it?
Professional opinions differ. Some say you should do it in a clockwise motion, and others say counterclockwise; some advise you to swirl the cup three times, others say seven. Do what feels right for you.

Reading tealeaves may sometimes feel like a Rorschach inkblot personality test. Each person looking into the cup will see a different image, and that's perfectly normal. However, if you are reading for someone else, keep in mind that only the reader should pick out the symbols and translate them. The reader is always more objective about the situation. This is why it may be better to read tealeaves for someone else and ask another fortuneteller to read them for you.

But, can I read my own teacup?
Of course you can. There's no harm in it. Just make sure you can be objective about it. In fact, once you start getting good at it, it might even be advantageous for you to read your own because you'll understand the symbols and how they relate to you.

Taking Note of the Details

Once you catch that first symbol, go on to a more detailed review of the teacup. Everything you will see somehow matters and carries meaning: what other symbols you note, where they are in the cup, and how they relate to each other. When you look inside the cup, symbols to the left of the handle represent the past; symbols to the right represent the future; and symbols around the middle of the cup represent events happening in the not-so-distant-future, in approximately three months' time. Symbols at the bottom of the cup are considered to be changeable and are also far away in time, from nine months on.

Symbols located near the rim of the cup are the most important. Any formations found on the uppermost part of the cup are considered to be good luck and good fortune. This is where your lips touch the cup, so it also relates to matters of the heart. Also, symbols near the top of the cup represent things happening close to present time: the present and immediate future. In other words, things on the rim to the right of the handle represent your near future, whereas things happening to the left of the handle refer to your recent past.

In general, if a symbol is closer to the handle, the problem could come from something within family or close to home. A symbol farther away from the handles signifies that the problem stems from something farther away from the person—outside his or her immediate circle of family and friends or something concerning work. Analyze the symbol at the bottom of the cup, see how it relates to the person's question, and decide what this means in terms of ill fate in the future. Then give your advice.

Common Tealeaf Symbols

Using both knowledge and instinct will help you understand the subtleties and nuances of the art of reading tealeaves. Think of it as music. A Beatles song isn't simply a string of notes. It's the composition of everything, the melody and the words together, that give the song intrinsic meaning. This is what creates that tune you hum or the chorus of a song that lingers in your mind and just won't go away.

Reading your teacup is the same. Look at all the symbols, shapes, and forms, and see what comes to mind as a general first impression, based on the person you're reading for and the question at hand. It's always better to relate everything together first and then look for the separate meanings in each cluster of tealeaves.

Keep in mind that tealeaf reading is a less defined divination art than the Tarot or astrology. Most psychics who read tealeaves use what they see in the leaves as a prop for their intuition and psychic abilities. For them, reading tealeaves enhances their understanding of the situation and is a wonderful aid in fortunetelling. At its best, tealeaf reading spurs on the senses.

ALERT!

Some readers say that symbols located at the bottom of the cup are of ill omen and bad luck. It may be wise to consider this as a warning. What are they trying to tell the querent? A symbol at the bottom may be a warning against mishap, job loss, or problems at home.

The Symbols Defined

Here is a list of the common symbols and their meanings, which have been derived by tealeaf readers over time. The interpretations presented here should be used for general reference. If certain shapes or figures have special meaning for you, you should absolutely tailor your reading to your interpretation of it, as long as you remain consistent.

Acorn: Financial success and improved mental and physical health.
Airplane: Career advancement or an upcoming journey.
Anchor: Near the rim it predicts stability and luck; near the bottom it represents a difficult situation that needs to be resolved.
Angel: Good news is soon to come.

Some psychics say that if you see an angel in the teacup, it cancels out any bad sign found in the rest of the reading. The angel is a powerful and pure symbol and can also predict happy times for matters of the heart.

Ants: Many difficulties that will, at the end, be overcome. Look to the other symbols in the cup to find the source of these problems.
Ape: Beware of people you trust—including yourself.
Apple: Long life, health, and achievement.
Arch: Upcoming travel or a new experience. If another symbol is located close to the arch, it will be directly associated with this interpretation.
Arrow: Bad news in love.
Axe: At the bottom, it represents difficulties; at the top, it brings news that difficulties will be overcome.
Ball: Ups and downs.
Bear: A period of transition.
Bell: News—good if at the top and unexpected if at the bottom.
Birds: A long journey is coming up.
Boat: Freedom and protection from harm. If it is near the top of the cup, it signifies a visit from a friend. Near the bottom, it signifies loneliness.
Bottle: Jealousy among colleagues at work. Advice is to "kill them with kindness"—the nicer you are, the further you'll get.
Bull: An impending fight with friends. Strength will be harbored in difficult situations.
Butterfly: Expected happiness—but be careful of fickleness.
Candle: Help from friends; concentration is necessary.
Castle: Protection against ill forces will come if you need it.
Cat: Beware of deceit or fickleness.

Chain: Relates to good news in matters of the heart and may predict a wedding engagement.

Chair: Expect an unexpected guest.

Cigar: A new friend.

Cigarette: A warning that tells you to concentrate more on career and less on foolish pursuits.

Circle: Completion of a project; success and luck. Gifts or money may be coming your way. A wedding engagement may be in the near future.

Clock: A sign of good health.

Clouds: A changed outlook to a problem is needed.

Clover: One of the luckiest of signs; happiness is sure to come.

Coin: Pertains to money and prosperity. If it is near the bottom of the cup, it is a serious warning against the dangers of losing money or becoming involved in a problem concerning it.

Compass: A lighthearted attempt to steer you in the right direction.

FACT

The symbols of tasseography are connected with symbols used in other divination methods, such as I Ching and astrology. Therefore, if you happen to see a sign for Gemini, the symbol "II," in your tealeaves, it may be that your answer has something to do with a particular Gemini (see Chapter 12 for more information on astrological sun signs).

Crown: Success that comes with the help of others. Someone is looking out for your well-being—possibly an older mentor.

Cup: A confirmation to the question asked—you're on the right path.

Dagger: Be careful what you say to people; a wrong word could get you into trouble.

Daisy: New love with someone you already know.

Devil: Karma and destiny.

Dog: A friend will test your loyalty.

Door: Strange events or happenings.

Dove: Always a lucky symbol, meaning peace, harmony, affection, prosperity, and love.

Eagle: Freedom and honor. A burden will soon be lifted.

Egg: Your fears are holding you back. Find courage and go for it.

Envelope: News—surrounding symbols will provide a further explanation.

Eye: Someone from your past is thinking or asking about you.

Face: In order to succeed, you need to define your goals more precisely.

Fairy: Someone is looking out for you—a spirit or a real-life mentor.

Fan: Fun, spontaneous times are soon to come.

Feather: You need to stop taking everything too seriously.

Feet: It may be time for a break from work.

Fence: Something or someone is holding you back.

Finger: Stop blaming yourself for everything. Recent past events were fated and could not be changed.

ALERT!

Getting the best results requires that you and the person you're reading for (the querent) believe in the power of divination. Doubt clouds judgment and shifts positive energy to negative energy.

Fire: A warning to stop being so selfish. You hurt others without realizing it.

Fish: Trust your intuition—it's strong now.

Flower: You'll start enjoying life as soon as you let yourself do it. Stop feeling sorry for yourself.

Fly: Setbacks are causing disappointment. Be patient and things will go as planned.

Forked line: You'll have to make a decision soon. Choose the simplest route.

Fountain: If you allow yourself to get hooked on beauty, it will cloud your judgment.

Fox: The next time you have a fight with someone, stop talking. Silence will get you out of this one.

Gate: See **Fence.**

Grapes: Spontaneity and fun are soon to come.

Guitar: Something from your childhood is blocking you from surging on ahead.

Gun: Fear of the opposite sex and/or trauma from your past; you may need to deal with your sexual anxieties.

Hand: You should stick to your morals. Going over the edge will only get you into trouble.

Hat: A new friend you'll make soon will turn out to be someone important in your life.

Head: A warning: Don't make a hasty decision. Think it over.

Heart: A new romance, or a warning that you're too involved in your current relationship. Does your partner feel the same way you do?

Horn: Prosperity; money coming from an unexpected source.

Horse: A loyal friend will come to your aid soon.

Horseshoe: Good luck and fortune are coming your way.

Ice cream cone: Let your playful side come out.

Jewel (gem): A warning against making enemies; be careful what you say.

Jewelry (necklace or bracelet): A secret admirer who is in love with you.

Key: You already know the answer to your question. Stop asking others for their opinion.

Kite: Pregnancy and fertility.

Knife: To find out the truth, look to your closest ally; also, be careful whom you trust.

You never know why something strikes you as it does; in the end, there's a reason behind everything. You just have to figure out what it is. And you'll get better at it with time. Glance at the other symbols to see how the one you're looking at fits in with the other meanings.

Ladder: Be patient—fate is guiding you.

Leaf: A turning point; things are about to change for the better.

Letter (of the alphabet): Refers to the first letter of a person's name; this person can help you or holds your heart.

Monster: You're setting up the same patterns for yourself; old habits need to be broken.

Moon: Trust your instinct and emotions—they're on the mark.

Mountain: Obstacles in your way are your own doing. Be patient and remove them one by one.

Mushroom: Disappointments you're experiencing are happening for a reason; you're learning something you need to learn. Take it gracefully.

Musical note: A spontaneous invitation will bring joy and happiness into your life.

Net: If it will cost you your pride, don't do it.

Numbers: Take note of the number and refer to the numerology chapter (Chapter 11) for an interpretation.

Octopus: You're getting involved in too many things at once. Slow down.

Oyster: Commitment; partnership; happiness.

Pear: Children and family issues; it's time to make sure everyone around you is okay.

Pentagon: You may feel that you're closed in and there's no way to solve the issue. Make a decision and stand behind it.

FACT

In divination, energy is channeled through the symbols, whether it is the shapes you see in tealeaves, the signs you read in Tarot spreads, or the numbers you derive through numerological calculations.

Pillar: Stop bearing all of the weight yourself. Get someone to help you.

Pyramid: You'll have a dream that contains prophetic advice. Take it.

Question mark: Patience is the only way you'll get through this. Hold tight.

Rat: A warning for your health. Take care of yourself.

Ring: A broken ring means troubles in love. A solid ring represents a new love or a step up for your relationship.

Saw: Keep your cool and your confidence. Things are getting better.

Scales: Justice, beauty, and harmony. Be fair in your dealings with others.

Scissors: A turning point; keep out of other people's affairs.

Shamrock: Always a sign of good luck.

Shark: Swiftness and action. You need to make a decision now.

Ship: Travel will benefit you now; you may meet a love attraction soon.

Snake: Danger. Be careful whom you trust.

Spoon: Wealth; money is coming your way.

Star: Your wish is on its way to coming true.

Straight line: Be patient. You're on your way to having what you want.

Sun: Joy, happiness, luxury. Spend some money on yourself.

Sword: You'll have to fight for what you want. It's within your reach.

Telephone: Communication problems in a love relationship.

Tree: Spiritual growth and rebirth.

Triangle: A three-way love problem.

Umbrella: A fortunate sign; clear skies are coming.

Vase: Domestic happiness; if it's near the bottom, it could indicate family problems.

Volcano: If you keep ignoring the situation, things will get worse. Take action.

Waterfall: What you desire will be yours.

Wishbone: When you see this in the teacup, make a wish.

Wolf: Beware of overly competitive colleagues or peers.

Woman: All is not as it appears.

As you try to recognize the symbols inside the teacup, be aware of your feelings. For example, if you suddenly experience a feeling of elation, or even a sense of dread, don't ignore it. Instead, write it down. After you've done that, close your eyes and concentrate on wiping your mind clean. Cancel your thoughts and center on being relaxed. This practice will help you do two things: It will keep you more focused on the task at hand and, after you've completed the reading, you can then relate the interpreted symbols back to the sensations you had moments before you started. Was your intuition trying to tell you something?

Chapter 15

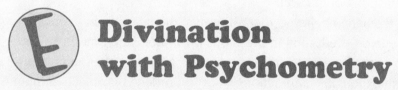

Divination with Psychometry

Everyone has heard about psychometry, but almost no one knows it by its proper name. Psychometry, in layman's terms, is a method of divination performed by touching an object belonging to a person, such as a ring or a watch, and then perceiving the events, circumstances, emotions, and even thoughts connected with the person and the object in question. In this chapter, discover the techniques utilized in this intriguing method of divination.

The Father of Psychometry

Although psychometric practices have existed since ancient times, psychometry received its name in 1842 from Joseph Rhodes Buchanan, an American scientist and physiologist. The term itself comes from the Greek *psyche* (soul) and *metron* (measure), so psychometry is "measuring of the soul."

Buchanan believed that all events, thoughts, and actions throughout time leave everlasting impressions on "ether" and that these impressions can never be erased or destroyed. He also held the belief that these events, thoughts, and actions were "recorded" on objects in nature, such as trees and rocks.

QUESTION?

What is ether?
Centuries ago, scientists and philosophers believed that while our world was composed of four elements (air, fire, earth, and water), the outer world or the heavens were made of ether—hence the term "ethereal": light, airy, spiritual, or of a "heavenly" force. Today, psychics use "ether" and "ethereal" to refer to something spiritual, such as an angel or the energy surrounding us.

Using Buchanan's work as a steppingstone, other psychometrists came to believe that each and every object has its own "soul"—like that of a living thing. The theory behind this is that each object has its own indelible memory. In other words, each object records every event that happens to it or around it.

Buchanan also conducted studies with other psychometrists and concluded that it was sometimes possible to diagnose an illness merely by holding the patient's hand. He did studies with his psychometry students and found that while each of them held a particular drug in his or her hand, he or she often showed symptoms as if the drug had been actually ingested. The same effect occurred, he concluded, when a psychometrist held the object of a person who was ill. The psychometrist would experience some of the same signs of illness as that of the ailing person who had held the object.

The object, Buchanan explained, recorded the suffering. Psychometry can also be used on important items and artifacts such as old manuscripts, fossils, and fragments of old ruins. Simply by touching them, the gifted psychometrist can describe, at length, ancient and long-forgotten civilizations.

Objects cannot lose their memory, but memories can be recorded over. In other words, the object will retain all past events, but the psychometrist will only pick up on the strongest memory—the most important event(s) the object has witnessed.

Clues to the Past, Present, and Future

Have you ever seen a movie or television story in which the police call in a psychic to help them solve a tough case? It happens more often than you may think. The police (as well as the FBI and other law enforcement agencies) frequently rely on certain psychics for help. The psychic receives photographs or personal items of the victim or a missing person, and from these personal effects he is able to provide clues that sometimes break the case. The stories vary, but all of them are astonishing.

You can also use psychometry in less dramatic circumstances. Most of the time, objects and places (entire buildings or separate rooms) carry with them information of the past and the present. Most psychics prefer divining with objects worn on an everyday basis. A watch, a ring, a bracelet, a necklace, or even a cigarette lighter will have a more interesting story to tell than, let's say, your pen. They may also use a hair band or sunglasses, but metal objects tend to work better, possibly because our bodies give off magnetic energy fields that are absorbed by metal objects.

Doing psychometric readings on people is another story altogether. People are imprinted with memories of the past, the present, and also the future. In other words, by touching the hand of a person, a gifted psychometrist is able to tune into the energy and "see" events that have not yet occurred. He or she can also pick up vibrations of people not yet met by the person who is being read.

Tuning In to the Energy

Certain people have stronger energy or vibrations than others, and the same is true of objects or places. To understand this concept, let's take a look at an example. Dominique has a watch from the 1930s. She has been wearing this watch for about six years now. And perhaps three other people have owned this watch before her.

Dominique hands over this watch to an experienced psychometrist. After meditating and holding the watch in his receptive hand, the psychometrist begins describing a horrific scene—one of bloodshed and terror. This, of course, has nothing to do with Dominique's life. With some research, it is discovered that one of the previous owners, also a woman, owned this watch for a very short period of time and that it was taken from her during World War II.

Objects are more likely to record turbulent, important, or drastic changes and events in history. Even though the woman who briefly owned the watch during the war may have carried it for less than a week, her imprint on the watch is the clearest of all.

You don't always have to touch the object in order to read the magnetic vibrations. Some gifted psychometrists can even read a person or an object from across the room.

Do You Have the Touch?

Some people have a natural talent for psychometry. Are you one of them? Have you ever picked up an object and received a flash of another image, one that was completely unrelated to the object itself? Most people ignore such visions, which rarely make any sense at all. The key is not to censor yourself; just allow the images to come forth. These images and feelings come to you for a reason.

It's possible that you, at one time or another, have touched an object or even a person and immediately felt either a very negative or positive vibe. In psychometry, as in all other forms of divination, you must trust your instinct and say the first thing that comes to mind. Without the presence of ego and the little rationalizations we make when we don't entirely understand the information presented to us, many of us have the ability to intuit events and circumstances.

FACT

It's believed that some blind people unknowingly develop skills in psychometry. They are able to sense things by touching a person, a letter, or an object previously owned by another.

Test Your Psychometric Abilities

Answering the following questions can help you decide if psychometry is a good form of divination for you.

1. Have you ever walked into a room and had a specific feeling about it? Maybe you wanted to leave right away, or maybe you felt the need to sit down and just lounge all day? When you enter a room you've never been in before, does it ever evoke an emotion of sadness or the feeling of warmth?

All rooms are filled with memories of thoughts and events that happened in them. If you're picking up the negative or positive energy, you're one step ahead of the game. A teacher once walked into a nursery room at the preschool where she was teaching. Once she stepped in, she immediately had the urge to leave. She felt a terrible sense of violence, sadness, and desperation. Of course, she didn't understand this strange reaction at all and was justifiably shaken up about it. The next day, with a bit of research, she discovered that the nursery room had, in fact, been a hidden war graveyard for soldiers hundreds of years ago. This preschool teacher was picking up the energy of a gruesome past.

2. Have you ever sensed, before you ever saw them, that a spouse or a friend had had a bad day?

Sure, it's easy to tell someone has had a rough day when you see them. But what about feeling or knowing something before they walk in the door—when they're just, let's say, walking up the steps or getting out of the car? This is energy you're tapping into, and it's a sure sign that your intuition is aiding you.

3. Have you ever known beforehand that the phone was going to ring?

Such occasions, which are not uncommon, go a long way to explain just how psychometry works. If you're skeptical, think about the telephone itself and how it operates. A century ago, the concept of electromagnetic waves flowing through the air would have been considered absurd. Now, you can be anywhere in the United States and call a friend in France or China from a cellular phone. If you've felt a vibe that the telephone is going to ring, you're tuned in to the energy waves.

4. Have you ever touched an article of clothing and had some sort of reaction to it?

It's very possible you were picking up an emotion from its owner. Clothes carry imprints of feelings and thoughts of every person who has worn them. Remember that favorite shirt you have from ten years ago, tucked away behind everything you own? You just can't seem to throw it away. When you pick it up, does it bring back emotions you felt around the time you used to wear it? Perhaps it brings back memories of people you spent time with or songs you listened to at that period in your life. When you finally give that shirt away, do you ever wonder who will be wearing it next?

QUESTION?

How did you do on the quiz?
If you've answered yes to any of these questions, or even if you're in doubt, read on. Anyone with a strong interest can master the basic skills used in psychometry.

Psychometric Divination

If you'd like to try psychometric divination for yourself, the first thing you need to do is to find your receptive hand. This is the hand that should receive the energy of the object or the person. Generally, your receptive hand is not your dominant hand; for instance, if you are right-handed, your receptive hand is your left hand (but, as always, there are exceptions).

To check, put your hands out in front of you, palms facing up—your hands should not touch. Without moving your left hand, move your right hand over your left hand (with your right-hand fingers perpendicular to the left palm). If you feel a slight tingling sensation in your left hand, the left is your receptive hand. Try the experiment reversed and see if you get the same feeling. If you try moving your left hand over your right and get the tingly sensation in your right hand, it means your right hand is the receptive one.

Exercising Your Skills

The next important step in mastering psychometric divination is to practice, practice, and practice. Here are some good exercises for you to try with family and friends.

ALERT!

Handle the object you are about to read very carefully. It's very important that you do not touch the object with your nonreceptive hand. If you use your nonreceptive hand, you risk getting a false reading.

Reading an Object

Have a friend sit in a chair next to you. Relax and clear everything from your mind. When you're calm and free of all thoughts, ask your friend to hand you one of her personal effects that's made of metal—like a ring, watch, or bracelet. It's better if the object is something your friend carries around all the time. Better still is an object that she has a strong emotional connection to. Make sure that your friend doesn't tell you any facts about this object. It's your job to figure these things out through a psychometric reading.

Take the object with your receptive hand and sit quietly for a few moments. Say the first thing that comes to mind—don't edit—whether it's a one-word association, a phrase, or a sentence. If the phrase "green door" comes to mind, go ahead and tell your friend. It may mean nothing to you but have some meaning for her. And there's nothing wrong with asking a few questions regarding words or visions that you see. Remember, it takes time and effort to perfect this craft. If it doesn't work the first few times, move slowly and keep trying.

Be aware of possible interferences. Always remember to take off your own jewelry or other metal objects before you begin. You don't want to confuse the magnetic energy or vibrations.

A Psychic Letter Reading

The next time you receive a letter from a friend, don't open it. Instead, taking care only to touch it with your receptive hand, sit down with the closed letter. Get out a tape recorder and start recording. After a few moments of meditation and relaxation, put the letter to your forehead and let it rest there for a moment. Feel the energy seeping into it. Some psychics call the place in the middle of your forehead "the third eye." You can use your third eye to tap into your intuitive senses.

Next, say out loud whatever comes to mind. Remember that you're not guessing, you're intuiting. For example, if you know facts about the friend who sent the letter, try not to use this information to "simply know" what he or she wrote you. Once again, don't rationalize. When you're finished saying everything that comes to mind, open the letter and read it. Then, you can play back your session and see if you were close to the mark. How did you do?

A Psychic Test

This exercise is often used to test psychic skills. Take out a deck of cards—you can use a regular playing card deck or the Tarot. Relax and clear your mind. Shuffle the cards and fan them out so that they're all visible, but face-down, on a flat surface. Think of a particular suit. Now pass your receptive hand lightly over the cards without touching them.

When you feel a tingly vibration, pick up the card you're most drawn to. How did you do? In the beginning, you can start with thinking of a particular suit. If you have some success with that, move on to thinking of a particular number. If you're really getting good, move on to guessing a specific card—both the number and the suit.

FACT

You may not always receive words when you do a psychometric reading. In fact, be aware of your emotions. If you suddenly have a wave of sadness sweep over you, it's possible that you're picking up the emotions that the person felt while writing the letter.

An Exercise for Novices

You'll need to have three boxes that are precisely the same (same size and color, with no identifying marks). The boxes must have lids to close them. Now choose a personal object from your room, preferably one that you touch often (and one with which you have an emotional connection). Pick one of the boxes and put this object into it. Close the lid. Make sure the lids are closed on the other boxes as well. Now go out of the room and have a friend mix up the boxes. They should be on the floor or on a table. When you come back, you should not touch the boxes.

Now, clear your mind fully and focus on the energy of this object. Slowly pass your receptive hand over all three boxes. One of the boxes should give you a surging, tingling sensation. This should be the box that contains your personal effect. Open it up. Did you get it right?

Touching the Future

You can also practice reading someone's future by utilizing some of the same techniques. Ask your friend to sit quietly next to you. Tell him to have a clear mind so that he won't project any wishes or desires on to you. Remember that you don't want to read his mind—you want to see actual visions of the future. It is possible that if your friend is thinking of an ideal future, you can pick up those details instead of getting a sense of real places and events.

Now take your friend's hand in your receptive hand. You should start seeing visions of this person, as if a movie were rolling in your mind. Remember not to edit. If you see this person with a purple alien, simply tell your friend, "I don't know what this means but we'll decipher it later." It could be a clue to something—a symbol or a strange allusion to something important.

Some psychometrists say that the Tarot is actually just a form of psychometry. By using the symbolism of the cards, the energy of the querent is channeled to the cards and then on to the reader.

Start out slowly and stay focused. If something confuses you, ask a question concerning it. For example, if you're getting visions of a baby next to a large house with a swing in front of it, ask your friend if he remembers such a place. It's possible that you're picking up energy from his past. If not, it could be a scene from his future.

The object is to get a good, valid reading. If you're not tapping into the energy on a particular day, or you're feeling a little off, you'll have difficulty getting a clear picture. It's better to wait until you're ready, even if you disappoint someone who desperately wants a reading, than to give a false or confusing interpretation. Even professional psychometrists have bad days when their intuition is blocked (think of it as a psychic writer's block). Limit your readings to when you feel good about doing them, and you'll be sure to get better results! Ⓔ

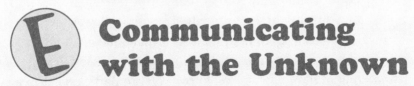

Chapter 16

Communicating with the Unknown

There are several methods of divination that are based on communication with other forces—ghosts, spirits, or other supernatural beings or entities—through such tools as the Ouija board, by conducting a séance, or even through automatic writing. This chapter will examine each one of these advanced methods and provide the information on how to use them correctly.

Mediums and Séances

What is a séance, anyway? Chances are, you are imagining a ceremony where a group of people sit around in a circle with their legs crossed, holding hands, and reciting incantations. The lights are dim, candles are burning, and one person is leading the session, waiting to be "possessed" by the ghost or spirit entity. Is that really how it goes?

Actually, you can conduct an actual séance this way, but there is no reason to sit cross-legged, hold hands, or recite incantations. And the leader of the séance, or the medium, is not "possessed"—we'll get to this further along in the chapter. You know you are participating in a séance if it's a ritual performed to make contact with the spirit world at a specific moment in time.

The Science of Séance

If you would like to conduct a séance, you will need a good location and a group of people interested in contacting the spirits. You will need no fewer than three people, plus one person who is willing to act as a medium. Don't allow nonbelievers to participate. The negativity of just one person may decrease your chances of success. A worse consequence, according to some psychics, is that inviting a nonbeliever exposes the séance to the less evolved of the spiritual entities. Also make sure that none of the participants is under the influence of drugs or alcohol.

Ideally, the séance should be held late at night, when fewer people are awake. However, avoid dark or threatening places. A séance should never be performed near a graveyard or near where someone died. You don't want the participants to be afraid—everyone should be open and relaxed. An uncluttered, tranquil, friendly, and airy setting is ideal. This location should have a round table that will accommodate only the people involved in the séance; avoid tables that would have empty seats once everyone sits down. Place one-color candles on the table— remember, each color vibrates at different frequencies and is used for tapping into different energies. If you have incense, that's fine, too, but place it somewhere else.

Before the séance, the group should perform a meditation of protection. And here is the final word of advice: Make sure your group is aware that there is no certainty that you will succeed in locating a particular spirit. Hope for the best, but realize that contacting spirits is difficult and that they may be needed elsewhere.

You can call on an angel or a spirit guide to protect you from negative influences during the séance. Using the method described in Chapter 5, ask everyone to imagine a pure white light flowing through them and throughout the room.

The Medium's Role

It's important to be careful when choosing a medium to conduct the séance. This person must be a trained and spiritually evolved professional. It's not enough for a medium to be a psychic. For successful channeling, a medium must have the right tools to attract spirits:

- A balanced spirit.
- Selfless, generous love to give.
- Receptivity and sensitivity.
- No old baggage, karma, obstacles, or childhood issues.
- Maturity and wisdom.

A good professional medium has learned to forgive and to love openly. Besides being psychic, she is a stable, balanced individual who has completely conquered her inner demons.

In Touch with the Spirit World

When you are conducting a séance, whom are you trying to contact? One answer is the spirit world. Spirits do not inhabit "space," so they can't possess the medium and take over his body. Instead, they are able to contact and influence the aura of the medium—that magnetic field of energy or glow that surrounds each person. Spiritual entities are able to speak to us through the aura of someone who knows how to hear them.

FACT

Your aura is pure when you are born, but it may be damaged during your lifetime with drug abuse, guilt, letting people treat you badly, and so forth. To cleanse your aura, you can meditate or rely on crystal or mind therapy.

If you can't get in touch with a specific soul or spirit, there are two possible explanations. First, we are very attached to our bodies and the material world. Everything here is dense and heavy compared to that which exists on the spiritual plane. Even though humans have access to the spiritual world, we are mostly a part of the real world and are more aware of it because we need to be in order to survive. Tuning in to the spiritual realm is not critical for our survival and we don't get much practice in it, so it's almost impossible for the average person to forge a contact with a spirit.

There is a second reason as well. There are many different planes in the spiritual world, and our world is one of the first levels. Compared with other planes, our concepts of time, space, relativity, and even reality, which mankind has constructed, are amateur at best. In other words, contrary to what we may wish, the spiritual world does not revolve around us—we are just one small part of it.

Many spirits do not wish to or cannot be contacted. They have moved on and are learning what their souls must learn now. The spiritual plane they are on is very far away (not in terms of space, but in terms of dimension) from ours. Consequently, professional mediums true to their trade will tell you that it is very difficult, if not impossible, to contact a specific soul or spirit. We do not normally choose our spirit guides or angels. They choose us.

Whom Do We Have Access To?

Unfortunately, spirit entities that are close to our plane are, many times, those who are lost, held back, or stuck in their own holding pattern. For some reason, they are still clinging to the beliefs they had on this plane and, consequently, refuse to move on. Some of them even refuse to acknowledge that they are no longer alive. In fact, many mediums say that confused spirits are usually the first ones to come through during a séance. They recommend that you ask the spirit (who claims to be so-and-so) to verify things that only the soul of the particular person would know.

Other than that, higher guides, spirits, and angels are available to us because they remain close to this plane. They're here to help us and they can sometimes come through as well.

ALERT!

Many times when spirits contact us, we don't perceive the information. Consequently, we don't even take notice. However, spirits are sometimes able to influence us without us knowing.

Divination Tool or Parlor Game?

Another complex method of divination that attempts to contact a spiritual entity is the Ouija board. In essence, when you are using the Ouija board, you are actually performing a séance. And we said before, a séance should only be done with a professional medium or an expert. Yet Ouija boards are available to anyone who can go down to the local toy store—it's on the shelves next to the board games.

There has been much controversy over the Ouija board since it first appeared. Some say it's a powerful paranormal tool, while others maintain it's nothing more than a parlor game. Many people still believe that the Ouija is evil. Most professional psychics don't agree with this. There is no such thing as evil spirits—though some may be capricious, confused, or even malicious. However, many psychics do believe that in the wrong hands, the Ouija board can be dangerous. You may invite lost or meddlesome spirits who won't want to leave into your house. Also, people do react in strange ways to fear, doing things they wouldn't normally do.

What does the term "Ouija" mean?
It's a brand name. According to one opinion, it was created by adding the French and German words for saying yes: *oui* and *ja.* The first known patent for the Ouija was filed in England in 1854.

Although anyone can use the Ouija board to contact spirit beings, it is always better to have a psychic medium present. Since there is no way to know how or if the Ouija really works, the mystery remains. But if you have doubts or fear, it's best to avoid it.

How the Ouija Works

Skeptics of the Ouija board say that, at best, the sitters (those using the Ouija) consciously or unconsciously steer the pointer toward specific letters. But in several experiments the sitters spelled out information they couldn't possibly know beforehand. The Ouija is, indeed, a mystery. So far, no one has been able to produce conclusive proof as to how or why it works (or doesn't work).

Professional mediums, psychics, and ghost hunters offer two different explanations for how Ouija boards work. One theory is that the spirits are able to pass on information through telepathy to the sitters' unconscious minds, thereby enabling them to involuntarily direct the pointer to the answers. The other theory holds that the spirits themselves move the pointers and the sitters are simply standing by, watching the process. Either way, the Ouija is not a game, a play tool, or a parlor trick, and should not be used as such.

Conducting a Ouija Session

If you do decide to use it, it's important to have a good reason and have all your questions prepared in advance. Be sure to review the section on conducting séances—all of that information should apply to using the Ouija board, except that you can have fewer than three people participate. Also, make sure that you don't conduct the Ouija séance over a bed or near the bathroom. (The bed is a personal place and may be inviting to spirits; conducting the séance near the bathroom is bad feng shui.) The best thing to do is use a table.

Be careful when choosing those you invite to participate; overemotional, nervous, fearful, or anxious people should never attempt to use the Ouija board. Love attracts love—the feeling when using the board should be one of projecting love and confidence in order to call and successfully connect with higher spiritual guides. Be sure that everyone is decorous and polite—don't interrupt each other or shout.

Some psychics suggest that the Ouija should be used in front of a shrine. If you have a protection symbol/statue in your house, you can pray to it beforehand and place the Ouija in front of it.

Let the Session Begin

To begin, perform a protection spell or meditation, as previously explained. The people involved should then place their hands lightly on the edge of the planchette, or pointer, which should move freely around the board. Keep in mind that if you're pressing down on the pointer, or if it makes a sound when moving, you're probably steering it. If you have successfully contacted a spirit, the planchette should move on its own. You should be barely touching it.

Once the session begins, psychics advise that you ask to communicate with an agreeable spirit who can keep the more confused, wandering ones away. It's always best to state up front what you are looking for from this contact. (If you don't know, you shouldn't be using the board.) Ask each question slowly, one at a time. The answers to the questions are then spelled out by the planchette, which points to letters, numbers, and Yes or No. Don't just assume a session is over when you feel like it. No one should get up and leave until you officially end the session by pointing to Goodbye (a word on the board).

If you do manage to make a connection with a spirit, the session can go on for hours. If the spirit wants to talk, you must hear it out. After all, you invited it. However, don't believe everything that's spelled out on the board. Remember, there are a lot of confused spirits out there.

Automatic Writing

Contrary to popular belief, automatic writing is not the process of letting your subconscious take over—it is not free-flow writing, in which you let the words flow onto the page without censoring or editing. Theoretically, automatic writing is when a spirit is actually influencing you (your aura) and writing the words through you.

Psychics of today say that automatic writing works just as well with a computer as it does with a pen and paper. In fact, automatic writing doesn't always refer to writing words. Some great works of art and music have been attributed to this complex method of divination as well.

FACT

Some people claim that they've felt the influence of two separate entities trying to write through them. If this happens, you should ask them to be patient and take turns!

In some cases, the words written by a person doing automatic writing are not in his usual handwriting. In other cases, people write down what looks like gibberish, only to discover later on that they have written something in a foreign language that they've never learned. And there are also cases in which automatic writing produces symbols that remain undecipherable.

No one can really say how automatic writing works. Some skeptics maintain that the people who claim to be writing with the help of a spiritual entity are simply tapping into their subconscious. They may be right, and if we all have a dormant genius within us just waiting to come out, it's a good thing! However, most professional psychics agree that there have been documented cases proving that this information could not possibly have come from the person's subconscious mind. One such case is the story of Pearl Curran.

Hard to Believe

At the beginning of the twentieth century, a Midwest housewife named Pearl Curran, who was neither well read nor interested in psychic phenomena, produced great works of literature as a result of automatic writing. Apparently, a spirit by the name of Patience Worth came to Pearl while she and her neighbor were playing with a Ouija board.

Through Pearl, the spirit wrote incredible novels and poetry that contained material Pearl alone could not have possibly known or guessed. Some of the books the pair wrote together include *Light from Beyond, Sorry Tale,* and *Hope Trueblood.* In this case, many researchers concluded, Pearl Curran was not being influenced—the books were actually written by the spirit.

ALERT!

Automatic writing is a serious undertaking, and should not be treated carelessly. Don't open the doorway to the spiritual world unless you are prepared to deal with the consequences—like the spirit of Patience Worth, who ended up with her own literary career!

Write It Yourself

If you're interested in trying automatic writing, remember that you should always do a protection/meditation ritual before you start. Visualize a pure, beautiful white light filling you. If you're feeling negative or distracted, postpone your session. If, however, you can sense the light surrounding you, protecting you with love, you're ready to begin.

Hold your pen (or pencil) very loosely. If you're using a computer, rest your hands lightly on the keyboard. You should be feeling open and relaxed. Clear your head of all thoughts. Think of nothing in particular except contacting a spiritual guide. It's best not to look directly at the computer screen or piece of paper; focus on something just to the left or to the right. Remember, you should not even be looking at what you're writing and you certainly shouldn't be trying to interpret it!

You may start experiencing a tingling sensation in your fingers and hands. This is an indication that it's working. If nothing is happening, you can ask your spirit guide a few questions. Start off with simple yes or no questions. You may even want to ask the spirit guide for its name. Most psychics suggest that you do not ask questions you want answered about yourself until later, when you're more familiar with your spirit guide.

QUESTION?

What happens if I write something crazy like "go jump off a bridge"?
Spirit guides never make a command or a demand. If you've written something like this, it's coming from your subconscious—not from a spiritual plane.

Once you start writing, everything should flow freely and naturally. Don't try to edit or analyze what it is you're putting on the page. Don't worry about grammar, typos, or even spacing. At the end of a session, you should not feel drained of energy. Thank your spirit guide for its time, help, and information. Know that you are once again in control of yourself completely.

Now, take a look at what you've written. Are there symbols, drawings, words that could refer to more than one thing? Work on trying to decipher it. Also remember that—as with every form of divination—you shouldn't go overboard. It may help to designate a couple of days of the month for doing automatic writing. If you feel comfortable with it, and it's not influencing you too much, you can step up your session time. Enjoy! Ⓔ

Chapter 17

Divining Love

One of the most tempting, wonderful things about divination is that you can use it to find out more about your love life. Professional psychics will tell you that the majority of questions thrown their way go something like this: "Will I get married?" "Is he my soul mate?" "Is she seeing someone else?" The list goes on. Divination is the best way to get a glimpse into your future when it comes to attraction, romance, and love. The methods are simple once you know what you're looking for. And, of course, practice goes a long way.

Destiny, Karma, and the Tarot

One of the basic questions people ask is whether a particular person is destined for them. The truth is that there are very few people in your life that you are destined to meet. And, sometimes, this person is not necessarily your soul mate, the one with whom you're meant to be forever. He or she could also be a life lesson.

In the Tarot, the Major Arcana are the cards of karma and destiny. Specifically, the one card that represents a destined soul mate and love is The Devil. If The Devil comes up during a regular reading, it does not have the "soul mate" significance. However, if you ask the particular question like "Is this (was this) destiny that we meet?" and you get this card, that's a karmic sign. If you are laying out a past, present, and future spread, note where The Devil appeared. If it's in the past, it may mean that it was someone you were meant to meet, but not someone who was meant to stay.

The I Ching can also help you determine which karmic phase of life (and love) you're in at this period in time. Numerology, too, can help you figure out your "personal year" love karma.

Gateways to Love

Your future is not set in stone, because the things you most desire (like love) won't happen until you're grounded, spiritually ready for them, and have learned a karmic lesson that will help you deal with actual success when you finally get what you want. There are gateways in life when the stars lean in your favor. The gateways align in a certain way and work (at times) to get you what you want—but you have to do the rest of the work. In love, divination is best used in order to find these gateways.

Astrology is probably the best method of divining when "the doors of love" will open to you. Runes and the Tarot can also indicate what can happen in the future—your possibilities in love—should you follow along the same path you're on at the time you cast.

If the Timing Is Right

Most methods of divination indicate things that are bound to happen in a matter of three or four months. (Of course, if you are not ready, there could be a delay of as much as two years.) To help you along, you can narrow down your questions specifically in order to figure out the timing of events. And you can also ask advice from the cards, runes, or I Ching on how you should go about making it happen sooner. Appropriate questions include the following:

1. Will I meet this person in the next two months?
2. What is he or she looking for in a mate?
3. How should I act?

Let's give an example with the Tarot. For the first question, you'll be looking for Major Arcana cards, which are fate cards, and also the Eight of Wands, which indicates swiftness. For the second question, you'll want to look at the specific meanings of the cards. If you come up with The Hierophant, for example, your soul mate is looking for a teacher. For the third question, you'll want to (again) examine the meaning of each specific card. If you come up with The Hanged Man, for example, it could mean patience, stalled time, or ego—you should wait for this person to come to you, or you need to flatter the person's ego.

Getting Hooked

The key to love divination is to avoid disappointing yourself. Unsatisfactory readings may lead to obsession or addiction. You'd be surprised how many people turn to divination for every action in life. Too much of any one thing is just not healthy. In love, divination is a fantastic tool for discovering possibilities, but wishing and desiring something does not always make it come true.

Did you know that some women actually leave their husbands because a psychic told them their husbands were unfaithful? You don't believe everything you read—so don't believe everything you're told!

You Can Turn to I Ching

The I Ching is an excellent method of divination to use if you want to examine your life's energy flows and to figure out where you're headed. In love, I Ching can tell you the underlying story of how a relationship is really going and it can give you excellent advice on how to cope with a current situation. And, of course, it can also give you advice for the future.

Remember that with I Ching, the questions you ask should be more general. Here are a few you can use in I Ching divination:

- What is the basis of our love situation at the moment?
- What's ahead for us in the near future?
- What's to be expected in the distant future?
- Why did I suffer so much in my previous relationship? What was my lesson?
- Is there a possibility for marriage right now?
- What is my partner's view on the relationship?
- Will I meet someone soon?
- Is there something I need to do in order to get myself more ready to meet someone?

The I Ching, as an oracle, helps put you on the right path. When you get an answer to one of these questions, make use of that advice and take steps toward changing your life so that these changes do in fact take place. Once you've started to make some positive changes, you can cast the coins again and ask the same question. Wait a good period of time before you do this (a month is an appropriate time span between readings).

Love This Year?

Let's look at an example of using I Ching to find out whether Alexander will meet his soul mate this year. As Alexander thinks of the question, you cast the I Ching coins six times. Then, you draw the hexagram and figure out that it's hexagram #64 (see Chapter 8). The description of the hexagram will give Alexander the answer to his question. The message seems to be positive—it's likely that Alexander will get what he wants.

Runes and the Way of Your Love

The runes are very much like I Ching. They're an oracle used for receiving good advice for your present situation. You can also use runes to show you your available gateways. In other words, you can determine from the runes what period you're in and how you can get to where you want to go.

Here is an example of how you can use the runes to ask a love question. Linda wants to know where her relationship is going. To answer her question, you can cast a past, present, and future spread by drawing three runes. The first rune you pick is the past, the second rune is the present, and the third is the future. Let's say you let Linda draw her own runes and she picks the following:

- **Past:** Thurisaz
- **Present:** Jera
- **Future:** Elhaz

As a confirmation or base for the situation, Linda picks one extra rune: Tyr. What does this all mean?

Thurisaz

As a past rune, Thurisaz indicates that Linda has probably been doing everything she can in terms of this relationship. Someone in her (or her boyfriend's) family has been trying to help out, too. Because this rune calls for knowledge and introspection and warns that hardship is expected, chances are that things are not going so smoothly right now. Fate is playing a part in everything. This rune also signifies that Linda has probably done her best in the situation, despite the obstacles she has had to face.

Jera

As a present rune, Jera can really mean two things. Because it is essentially a harvest rune, it means you will reap what you sowed. In other words, if you've been giving and giving in a relationship, it's time to receive your reward. Jera also refers to the end of something, including a love relationship. Unfortunately, it could mean that Linda's efforts are for naught. But, fortunately, it means that this breakup may lead to a new, better period for her.

QUESTION?

What should I be looking for in a past, present, and future spread?
You'll want to look more closely at the past and the future. These two facets (more than the present) will help you determine the way things are going.

Elhaz

Linda picked Elhaz as her future rune. Regarding the future, this rune has neither a positive nor a negative connotation; perhaps the future of this love relationship is not yet decided. But one thing is sure: It indicates that the querent (Linda) should not get too tied up (or emotionally involved) regarding the situation. She can prevent disaster by having an open mind and seeing the truth. Chances are, the end result of this situation will not be marriage and family.

Many times oracles (such as runes or the I Ching) give you a general sense of what you can do in order to improve your situation. If a professional psychic is too specific, you may want to question whether he is exaggerating the information.

Tyr

Though Linda's three runes were essentially clear in their explanation of the situation, there may be times when you want to pick an extra rune in order to clarify your response. In essence, the Significator or base rune says that Linda should not try to control things, or they will backfire.

What is going to happen will happen—and that may be good news or bad news. In either case, Linda should have the strength and courage to face the future.

Discerning Feelings with Tarot

For discerning feelings of others toward you regarding love, friendship, or business, your best bet is to use the Tarot. Keep in mind that the Tarot picks up energy at the present time, and feelings do change. The secret to utilizing the Tarot for love feelings is simple: Be very specific. You can ask many different questions that almost sound the same but, in reality, are not similar at all. Here are some examples:

- How does my boyfriend feel about marriage in general?
- How does my girlfriend feel about marriage with me?
- How does he feel about me?
- How do I truly feel about him?
- Is this relationship on the right path?
- How does my ex feel about me?
- Can I trust my girlfriend to be faithful to me?
- Does my boyfriend still have feelings for his ex?

Here is a sample reading for Tarot. To answer Jessie's question, "How does he feel about me?" we did a complex past, present, and future spread (see Chapter 6). The cards came out in the following order:

1. Ten of Swords
2. The Moon
3. Three of Cups
4. Two of Cups
5. The Lovers
6. The Fool
7. Five of Pentacles
8. Eight of Wands
9. Three of Swords
10. The Hermit

Let's go through the columns of past, present, and future one by one and decipher how Jessie's boyfriend, Kevin, feels about her (at this moment in time).

ALERT!

Don't forget to remind the querent (or yourself) that feelings can really change fast, depending on actions taken or not taken. The cards only show the direction in which things are going right now! If you want, you can also ask the cards for love advice.

The Past

The Two of Cups is the ultimate love card. Kevin absolutely loved Jessie. The Fool means he was taking a risk *or* that he was head over heels in love *or* that he was wrapped up in the moment. The Eight of Wands means that things went fast in the relationship *or* that these cards indicate the very recent past/present.

The Present

The Three of Cups says Kevin still feels joy with and affection for Jessie. The Ten of Swords indicates that there has been a break or a change in Kevin's feelings *or* in the relationship. Did they break up? The Moon indicates that he is feeling emotional about the present love situation with Jessie *or* it could also mean that he is obsessing about the problem. The Hermit indicates patience *or* alone time. This could mean that he feels he needs time by himself *or* that he feels alone or lonely. It could also signify that he's handling the situation with caution.

The Future

The Lovers card in the future indicates that, whether or not they break up, they will have love feelings and/or sexual intimacy again. The Five of Pentacles indicates that Kevin will soon have anxiety over his feelings for her *or* over her feelings for him. The Three of Swords (heartbreak, regret) in the outcome future position does not bode well for the relationship. But it could mean one of three things:

1. His feelings change and he breaks off with her.
2. She breaks up with him and he's heartbroken.
3. He regrets something deeply that he's done in the relationship.

FACT

Other love cards to look out for: Four of Wands (marriage; change of address; stability); Nine and Ten of Cups (love and joy; Ten can also mean marriage); Ten of Pentacles (financial stability in love).

The Conclusion

Notice that the cards hint at certain things but they don't tell the whole story. You'll want to ask Jessie more questions to understand what exactly the cards are referring to. For example, if the two are broken up, the cards spell out something entirely different than if they are still together. Now is the time to go deeper and ask more specific questions. The Tarot is very effective when it comes to the matters of the heart. Ask good questions and you'll get good answers.

Chapter 18

The Future of Your Career

While questions of love are the most popular, the second most inquired-about topic in divination is career. Questions about a current job, career path, and possible achievements are high on the list for everyone. Should I take this job? Should I go back to school? Can I afford to take the summer off? In this chapter, discover the best ways to find out what the future holds for you in terms of your work.

Should I Take That Job?

This is perhaps the most common question regarding careers, and it's no surprise—accepting a new job offer will have a big impact on your life, both in the near future and over the long run. Most obviously, it will influence the course of your career, but it will change your life in other, subtler ways as well. New people you meet, ideas you will be exposed to, and a million other factors will take you on a totally different life path. Before you make that decision, why not check what the future may hold for you? In the end, of course, the decision is left up to you, but divination can be a helpful guide in your search for the right answer.

Consider your main reason for getting a new job. Are you looking for a higher position, or more recognition or money? Are you switching jobs for convenience? Or is it because you are eager to leave your previous job? Once you have the answers, it will be easier for you to figure out what will make you happy in your next job.

You can use runes, the Tarot, or the I Ching, but you will have to break down this question into more specific questions. From the combined answers you can then make your decision. Here are some examples of specific questions:

- Will I get along with my new boss?
- Is there room for moving up?
- Will I be happy with this kind of work?
- Will I get along with my new colleagues?
- If I pass up this job, can I be happy for now in my present job?
- If I don't take the job, will there be a better opportunity in the near future?
- Will I get satisfaction in my new work?

The point is, you don't want your questions to be open-ended. Try to get to the heart of the matter. If you ask specific questions, you'll get specific answers.

The Threat of Job Loss

Another important question that may one day come up is "Will I lose my job?" Let's take an example. Jane works at a large company. In the last few weeks she's heard rumors of downsizing, so she decides to talk to her boss, Alice. Alice tells her that a few senior executives would be coming in next week to review the department. If they're not completely convinced of the department's value to the company, they may get rid of it entirely.

As you can imagine, Jane really wants to know if she's about to lose her job, but this is a difficult question—it involves many people, their decisions, and many other factors. Unless it's the fate of this company to get rid of Jane's branch this year, or Jane's personal karma/fate to lose her job now, the answer can change depending on all of the people who play a role in making this decision.

Still, it doesn't hurt to try to see what the future has in store for Jane. In this case, it's best to rely on Tarot to get the clearest answer. Or, you can use the I Ching and runes to get some advice and to help you understand why things are moving the way they are. You can also ask the I Ching about the general state of the branch/department Jane is in.

Let's Go with Tarot

First, Jane tries a quick three-card future spread. As she shuffles the Tarot, she thinks about her question: Will I lose my job? Then, she picks three cards:

1. Present/near future
2. Future (from two weeks to one month)
3. Future (one month or more)

FACT

In the quick three-card future spread, the time distinctions are not always clear. They are estimated time frames that will help you figure out the consequence of events and give you a rough idea of what to expect.

In Jane's spread, the three cards are The Hermit, The Chariot, and Seven of Swords. What does this mean? First of all, Seven of Swords is never a good sign as an outcome card. And the other two cards are from the Major Arcana, which means that these events are surely tied in with fate and karma. The Hermit means that Jane is in a waiting period and she must be patient—there's not much she can do to help the situation. The Chariot can signify two things: good news or travel. Does Jane have a trip coming up? If not, she'll have some sort of good news regarding the situation coming her way. The Seven of Swords stands for betrayal or false words. But in this spread, it's difficult to tell whom the betrayal or false words are coming from. Does Jane betray herself? Does the company betray her?

Asking Another Question

Since the answer isn't clear, Jane can do another spread and ask a different question. When you're deciding what kind of question to ask, it sometimes helps to think backwards. For example, what type of outcome cards signifies business success? Well, we already know that the Four, Six, Nine, and Ten of Pentacles stand for money, security, and stability. Now, what question would refer to this kind of answer?

Jane decides on this: "Will my department have stability or problems in the next three months?" To get an answer, she lays out a three-card past, present, and future spread, and gets the following results:

- **Past:** Five of Pentacles
- **Present:** The Tower
- **Future:** Six of Pentacles

The Five of Pentacles, which frequently signifies anxiety and problems with money, is not referring to Jane but rather to the department itself. This means that the department was probably experiencing financial issues in the recent past. The Tower card in the present column signifies that everything is changing and breaking apart. This could also be referring to the current state of the department due to the problems and worries of its people. However, the Six of Pentacles, which means success with money affairs, says that this situation is bound to have a good outcome. Therefore, the department will have financial security in the next three months.

> Keep in mind that the Six of Pentacles is a Minor Arcana card, which means that this is the way things are going now but the situation may change. Chances are, though, that things are going to be just fine for Jane.

A Good Day for a Presentation

While some career-related questions have to do with big changes such as losing or getting a job, you will also need divination to help you with everyday kinds of decisions. One such decision is picking an auspicious day for an important presentation or meeting. The truth is, if you're prepared and you feel good about the presentation you're going to make, any day is as good as the rest. Divination can only show you the days when luck is on your side for your maximum success. For this kind of a question, it's best to turn to numerology, which can show you when your luck will work for you and not against you.

> Don't ever let divination sway your confidence. It's supposed to help you. If you have a presentation slated for a certain day, and then you see that the numbers are not what you'd hoped for, don't despair. Numerology is not the end-all of fate—you are.

To check a particular date, all you need to do is add up the numbers of the month, day, and year (see Chapter 11). Let's take a look at an example. David has an important presentation on January 28, 2004. Will it be a good day for his presentation?

First, let's add up all the digits: 1 + 2 + 8 + 2 + 0 + 0 + 4 = 17. Then, add up the two digits again: 1 + 7 = 8. If you look up the interpretation for 8 in terms of work (also in Chapter 11), you'll see that David is in luck. The number 8 is the perfect business prophecy number.

Dealing with Colleagues

You know your colleague is up to no good, but you don't know if it's your place to say something. Now is a perfect time to consult with divination. Either I Ching or the runes can give you good advice—and your instinct will be useful as well. If your colleague is doing something that is hurtful to others (or against the law), it may be time to speak up regardless of the divination results you get. If he or she is just getting ahead by "unorthodox" means, on the other hand, maybe now is not the right time for you to draw attention to yourself.

Let's take an example. Steven works for a law firm, as does his colleague and friend, Fred. Lately, Steven notices that Fred is always taking extra-long lunches. It's possible that Fred is meeting with prospective clients, but it's more likely that he's slacking off. Should Steven say something? It may be better if Fred's dedication to the company (or rather, the lack of it) is out in the open.

Steven is torn, and he decides to ask the runes for advice. As he casts a simple past, present, and future spread, he forms the question: Should I say something about Fred? Here are the results:

1. **Past:** Lagaz
2. **Present:** Raidho
3. **Future:** Wunjo

Interpreting the Spread

Now, look up the meanings of these runes in Chapter 9. As you can see, the first rune aptly describes the recent past and present. The situation is not really under Steven's control. The advice is that he should accept what is happening and go with the flow. Because this rune advises Steven not to punish himself, it probably means that Steven is either blaming himself for not telling someone at work or feels bad for wanting to tell. This rune is basically telling him to let the situation go and not feel guilty about anything.

FACT

Because Lagaz also refers to luck, it could mean that this problem is actually bringing luck to Steven. It's possible, for example, that the higher-ups are already well aware of the situation and are impressed with the work Steven is doing to compensate for his colleague's absences.

The interpretation of the second rune, Raidho, should be clear as well. It's better to stay away from the situation—to let go and move on. It also signifies that it may be a good time for travel. Does Steven have an opportunity to get away? If so, he should try to use it to his advantage. Since this rune also refers to people of his past, it's possible that he may run into someone soon who has a direct influence on him regarding the question/situation. Either way, this rune is saying that Steven shouldn't make any sudden moves at the moment (except, of course, to get as far away from things as he can).

Finally, Wunjo as a future rune indicates a very positive outcome. Good things are ahead—Steven will receive success or reward for his achievements and hard work. Notice that this rune only refers to Steven. In other words, there is no information on what will happen to Fred. But the really important thing about this rune is that it refers to shedding light on matters that were previously difficult to discern. Therefore, whatever problem Fred's absence at work was causing Steven—perhaps weighing down Steven with extra work—it will vanish in the near future.

This reading seems pretty clear: Steven should just go about his business. Everything will turn out okay, as long as he does absolutely nothing.

When It's Time to Take a Break

Everyone needs a vacation; the real question is—is this the right time for one? If you want to do a Tarot spread to find out, there is only one card that decisively indicates travel: The Chariot. If you do a spread and The Chariot comes out in the future column and with good outcome cards, then you're set. Unfortunately, you're praying for a miracle—waiting for one card out of seventy-two. The solution? First, try it anyway. If you get The Chariot card with unfortunate outcome cards, then you absolutely shouldn't go. But if the Chariot card does not come out, simply ask another, more specific question.

> If you are not sure how to formulate your question, think of a "feelings" question. In this case, since the question "Should I take a vacation?" is too general, ask, "Will I have a positive experience if I take a vacation now?" Feelings are much easier to read in the cards.

Narrowing Down Your Query

Let's say that Sandra asks, "Will I be happy taking this vacation?" Actually, this question isn't specific enough either. What does "happy" mean for Sandra? Does it mean that she wants to be tranquil, and left in peace? Or does it mean, perhaps, that she'd like to meet someone?

Upon further inquiry, Sandra says that she really wants to get away because she needs a break from work and she'd love to have a fun, amorous fling—if she finds someone with whom she really connects. So how about asking this: "Will I meet someone on this vacation and will I have fun?"

The Tarot Spread

To get an answer, Sandra laid out a ten-card past, present, and future spread. Here is what she got (refer to Chapter 6 for what the spread should look like):

1. Death
2. Nine of Swords
3. The Moon
4. Two of Cups
5. Knight of Swords
6. King of Pentacles

7. The Lovers
8. Ten of Wands
9. The Empress
10. The Fool

An experienced Tarot reader would have a field day with these cards. There's a lot of information here—and even a few warnings. The reader will have to ask Sandra a few personal questions in order to translate all the cards correctly. Let's get started.

FACT

If Sandra is deciding between two different vacations, she's going to have to ask two separate questions, one regarding each destination. For instance, if she's still deciding between taking a vacation so she can visit her mother and going to a luxury spa village in Hawaii, she'll have to say which vacation she's talking about.

The Past Column

Though Sandra's question is about taking a vacation, the other underlying question is about meeting a man. And even if it weren't, these three past cards indicate a relationship. You've got the Two of Cups, the love card, right next to the King of Pentacles, signifying an older man. (On rare occasions, this can also refer to a member of Sandra's family such as a father or an older brother.) Then you have the Ten of Wands, which usually refers to oppression or opposition. Did Sandra have a relationship in the recent past? Perhaps she had one that was held back by opposing forces (work, family) or one in which she was holding back for other reasons? Or is she, perhaps, still in a relationship and the rapport is currently stalled? Let's look at the next column.

The Present Column

The Moon stands for emotions and/or obsession. Ask Sandra more questions. Is she or her ex suffering from a relationship? And if there was no past relationship, this could refer to Sandra's obsession with simply getting away. The Death card, which is the background of the whole story, the Significator card, signals drastic change. This could refer to Sandra's change of heart or changing the way she looks at things, regarding the question. The Nine of Swords means cruelty or harsh emotions. Is Sandra mentally chastising herself or is someone doing that to her? The Fool means taking a leap of faith. Perhaps this is referring to Sandra getting away and going on vacation. Therefore, we should view the future cards as the answer—what will happen if Sandra goes.

The Future Column

The future cards, if Sandra goes on this vacation, are obvious. You have the Knight of Swords, The Lovers, and The Empress. The Knight of Swords refers to a man Sandra will meet in the future. The Lovers implies that Sandra and this new man will become sexually intimate. The Empress can mean two things. Since The Empress often refers to fertility and motherhood, this could be stating (or warning) that, from the union of the two, a baby may be conceived. Other than that, the Empress can refer to nurturing qualities, which means that Sandra could feel tenderness toward this man, or that he'll make her feel like a woman.

The Conclusion

The future outcome is clear. Yes, Sandra should go on vacation—she'll have a great time! And yes, she'll meet someone if she wants to. Ⓔ

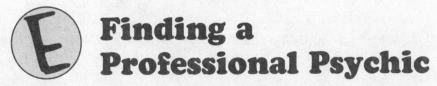

Chapter 19

Finding a Professional Psychic

By now, you should be able to perform divination on your own, but perhaps you are not comfortable divining for yourself, or you'd like to get some tips from professionals. In either case, you may want to find a psychic who would do a reading for you and answer your questions. But how do you go about locating someone good and avoiding impostors? This chapter will help you discern between the genuine psychic and the fraud.

Street ("Gypsy") Psychics

Unfortunately, most people have their first "professional psychic" experience with a "gypsy" fortuneteller. Why? Because they seek you out. They're outside on the sidewalks with little tables set up, replete with candles, incense, and cards—with nothing to offer but their instinct, common sense, and trickery. They lure you in by saying, "I have something to tell you," and then they go about guessing what it is that's ailing you. Or they tell you that something terrible will happen to you soon if you don't let them help you. Apparently, they say, they see it in your eyes.

But what is it that these people are really after? The answer is simple: They need your money. Stay away from psychics who go looking for you. A real psychic will be sought out for her abilities; most "street psychics" are only looking to pay the rent.

A gypsy psychic is any street psychic who is trying to make a quick buck from any unsuspecting passersby and may even give you a false reading. This term does not refer to the Gypsies as a people.

Lured into It

You are walking down a street when you are accosted by a woman. "I have something to tell you," she says. "You have a brother, no?" You shake your head. "A sister?" You say yes. "Ah, of course. A sister. She is in grave danger. Come with me and I will show you." At this point you're skeptical. But you have half an hour to burn and as you start walking away, you feel guilty. What if your sister really is in trouble? It can't hurt to hear what the woman has to say. So you go with her.

One hour and fifty dollars later, you've been told that you're very sensitive, honest, good-hearted, generous, instinctive (no one can put something past you!), witty, charming, interesting, romantic, outgoing. Ah, but she knows you so well. Basically, you're paying to receive flattery and compliments. And it is possible that a street psychic has the gift. The problem is that when money (and desperation) come into the picture, you can't trust what the street psychic has to say to you. Chances are, she's more preoccupied with her own situation than she is with yours.

Saved from a Curse

Needless to say, gypsy psychics don't have the means, the skill, the talent, or the inclination to give a good, honest reading. They'll lie in order to get more cash from you; one common trick is to tell you that someone placed a curse on you and that they'll remove it for a small fee. Of course, they claim that their compensation is insignificant compared with how much better your life will be.

The curse will always refer directly to whatever the psychic intuits is your most important question. If, for example, most of your questions are about love, the gypsy psychic will tell you you're going to break up soon if you don't remove the curse someone has placed on you. Or, if your questions are about your mother, who is ill, the psychic will tell you that your mother will not recover until you have the curse removed.

Try as you may, this curse thing has got you shaken up. So you pay the extra hundred or two hundred dollars just to ease your fear. But is there such a thing as a curse? Let's say you accidentally bump into the gypsy psychic and she drops her bag of groceries. Although you try to help her pick everything up, she stares you down and gives you "the evil eye." Does this mean that tragedy and suffering will befall you? And how do you remove a curse?

The answer is simple—you remove it by not believing in it. Curses only work because people give them credence or power. They simply aren't real. Don't let someone draw you into this ridiculous absurdity. Curses exist only in your mind.

Psychic Phone Lines

Talk about convenience. You can pick up the phone and talk to a psychic from the convenience of your home. Plus, the first three minutes are free—what could be better? Psychic hotline numbers are advertised everywhere—in magazines, on television, in newspapers. Why are they so popular? Because there are a lot of people out there looking for answers.

But can you get a good reading over the telephone? Yes and no. There are two types of telephone readings: the person on the other end of the line may be a professional psychic—or an unemployed actress looking to make extra money on the side. Think about it this way: There are too many psychic hotline numbers and psychics out there for them all to be the genuine article.

Because you are charged by the minute, psychics are encouraged to keep you on the phone for as long as possible, and to keep you calling back again and again. And before you know it, your phone charges are astronomical. Did the phone psychic mention debt as one of the problems you would face in the future?

ALERT!

Check around and compare the fees. Keep in mind that higher prices do not necessarily mean better quality. There are many good psychics out there who don't charge a lot.

Not Always a Sham

It is entirely possible to get a good psychic reading over the phone. If you've met a psychic and know that this person is a professional, you can call him and have the reading done over the phone. Psychics will tell you that it's always better to have the querent within reaching distance, but a phone reading can be surprisingly accurate.

Similarly, if you trust a good friend's recommendation, you can call a psychic whom you've never met. Find out as much as you can about this person. Is he fanatically religious? This could pose a problem. You can also find books and articles written by or about specific psychics. If they have a Web site, read all of the information. This should give you a clue as to what their methods/beliefs are. One word of advice here: Don't just blindly accept the truth of testimonials; they may be disguised publicity.

Cyber Psychics

Surprisingly enough, there are actually some good, accomplished psychics to be found on the Internet. You can even do a search on the Web for what interests you in particular. Often, it isn't difficult to differentiate between which psychic Web sites are real and which are made by some self-proclaimed witch working out of her kitchen in Nebraska.

If a psychic site declares that it's the "original" psychic Web site, or the only one that can help you, beware. Also, be careful of the psychic who calls himself the only original, "real" psychic. In our experience, the words "true," "best," and "genuine" are more frequently used by charlatans than by professional psychics. Of course, professionals need to promote themselves as well, but just keep in mind that a psychic who claims to be the one and only psychic who can help you is probably a fraud.

Like a good medium, a good psychic is a clairvoyant-cum-psychotherapist. Even if you don't believe in divination, the genuine Web sites offer you practical, sound advice geared toward helping you lead a more spiritual, mentally healthy life.

Take Advantage of the Resources

Some Internet sites post sample readings as well. These are quite good because you'll get an idea of the kinds of questions you can ask, how long the readings are, and so on. Also, look at the readings—are they vague? Do they apply to everyone? Or do they contain rare, genuine information?

Many Internet sites are broken up into different categories: dreams, love, career, and so on. You can pick your own subject and, while you're at it, decide which psychic from the particular site you'd like to do your reading. If they have sample readings with the different psychics, read all of them and decide which psychic's style is to your liking. Some sites also offer group readings, which are two or three separate readings done by two or three different psychics. Group readings can be very helpful because you get extra advice and opinions from more than one psychic.

Psychic Readings by E-mail

Today, you have the opportunity to get a psychic reading or a question answered via e-mail. Does that sound silly? It's not. Even professional psychics have discovered the convenience of offering readings through the Internet. Although there are a few generic, uninteresting, and perhaps even misleading psychic Web sites out there, it's not unheard of to have an excellent reading this way.

In fact, one great thing about the Internet is that it enables you to get a reading from a good psychic who lives thousands of miles away from you. It also gives the psychic time and careful consideration to write you out a full detailed report of things to come. Plus, if you save the e-mail with your reading, you can go back to it months later and check its validity.

How It Works

Getting a psychic reading via e-mail is simple. You go to the psychic Web site and state your questions—mention as many details and information as you like. The more specific your questions, the more focused your answers will be. Then, you're transferred to a secure server page to provide your credit card information. (Be sure you check to make sure that the server is secure.)

In response, you should get a detailed psychic reading. The Web sites listed in Appendix A will provide you with pages and pages of precious, specific information on future events. Most of these psychics will answer back in a timely, very professional manner—with predictions as well as philosophic tidbits to really make you think. A good psychic is always a natural therapist and will offer positive feedback and advice on various ways to solve any particularly nagging problem. At the very least, you'll have an outside, objective opinion.

Some psychic Web sites also offer free follow-up questions and answers. It's like getting two readings for the price of one, which can be especially advantageous when you're not sure of a response you've been given and would like it to be clarified.

ALERT!

Make sure to limit yourself. If you receive some practical advice, use it. Don't look for yet another site to give you more insight. Remember to get out there and live your life. Nothing will happen if you're just sitting home waiting for your e-mail psychic interpretations to arrive.

Psychic Advice from Friends

Do you have a friend who knows how to read cards or runes? Perhaps he learned it from his grandmother, or from his strange, interesting next-door neighbor. Well, guess what—sometimes a friend can read your cards just as well as a professional. You don't always have to pay in order to get a good reading. In fact, friends are sometimes your best bet. Make sure that it's someone that you have a good feeling about, or someone with whom you feel a connection. And be sure that you trust his divination skills.

A reading by a friend isn't done for money—it's done only because he cares about you, and that's the best kind of reading. And time isn't an issue either, so your friend can take as little or as much time as necessary.

The only problem with having a friend reading your cards or intuiting your situation is that he knows you too well, and his judgments may interfere with how he interprets the results. Keep in mind that it's difficult to remain objective while doing a reading for someone you know. And it's all too easy for someone to use the information they're aware of in order to fill in the missing blanks.

In addition to doing a reading, a friend may also help you find a good psychic. If you trust your friend's judgment, count yourself lucky. A suggestion from a friend you respect is worth ten times more than a random testimonial offered on any Web site.

Gentle Guidance

Another benefit of having friends do readings for you is that they'll stop you if you get indulgent. It's normal to get excited over a positive reading you've received from a friend about love, career, or a life change. But friends will be the only ones to tell you that you're concentrating too much on the readings and too little on your life. Of course, all psychics are willing to help you upon payment of a cash advance. A friend is the one who'll tell you that you've crossed the line.

The calmer you are about a crazy situation, the better things will go for you. Being in a rush will not help you solve the problem. Have faith that things will turn out for the better if you trust in time and in energy. Knots or problems that are extra tight take time to unravel. And you'll still be there when they finally do. (E)

Chapter 20

Changing
Your Future

You've practiced some divining on your own and have even had a professional psychic reading done, but you don't like the results. You now know that the future is not set in stone, but aren't quite sure how to go about changing it. Well, it's not as difficult as you may think. To bring about a positive future, nothing works better than plain old-fashioned wishing. In this chapter, find out how to make your deepest wishes actually come true.

Self-Discovery and Visualization

Changing the future is about knowing what you want. We all think that we know what we want. But do we really? Think about it. Have you ever been wrong? We all have. The truth is, we always think we know what we really want, when in reality, many of us have no clue as to what would truly make us happy in any given situation. This is where divination, wishing, meditation, and fate come in handy. Your future is as good as you want to make it. If you're waiting for a psychic to tell you that everything is going to be okay, it may be an indication that there is something wrong in your life that you need to fix. And the only one who can help you to do that is you.

Divination can't change the future for you; you have to shape it and make it happen. Wishing puts your ideas out there and helps guide the energy to work in your favor.

The terms "self-discovery" and "visualization" may seem foreign to some people. In fact, they're very simple—and very important. Self-discovery is not about traveling around the world, tasting strange foods, or trying out a new sexual orientation. Self-discovery is finding out what makes you happy, and this is not the simplest thing to do. It takes courage to love and accept who you are. And many of us have not mastered it.

It's about Making Choices

The truth is that divination can help you to make choices when you know what options you have. If you're constantly weighing yourself down with people around you who don't really add anything to your overall happiness, your outlook on life will become muddled. And it's that much more difficult to clear the path in order to make way for new, positive experiences and forge ahead. Stop being a martyr! If your so-called friend is constantly putting you down and you don't have the guts to cut her out of your life, think of this: There are other people in the world looking to punish themselves. Let this woman find them. In order for you to spiritually and mentally evolve, you'll have to make choices for yourself.

ALERT!

If you think that having one negative influence around you is not a big deal, think again. It's better to have no friends at all than one close friend who feeds off your positive energy.

Meditation on the Tarot

All methods of divination are connected, and many of the symbols are universal, representing something much bigger than themselves. The twenty-two Major Arcana images of the Tarot refer to phases in life from birth to death. By choosing one card to meditate and wish on, you can connect with so much more than a simple picture. The following sections explore how you can use some of the Major Arcana cards for meditation.

ESSENTIAL

Besides wishing or meditating on one card, you can also create a spread (such as past, present, and future) that expresses and indicates a desired outcome of a situation. When you meditate on a specific spread, you're telling the universe what you want.

The Sun

If you're just wishing for better things ahead, The Sun is your best bet. Simply take the card in hand, take a few deep breaths, and imagine the world as you would like it to be. The Sun brings luck as well as good karma, positive aspects, and important realizations into view.

The Fool

Although this card could be a warning that you're throwing too much caution to the wind, it's also the perfect meditation card for someone who is too sensible. The Fool is a good card to wish on and meditate with in order to bring spontaneity back into your life after you've lost it by experiencing a particularly rough period. It's the card to wish on if you'd had problems in the past with taking risks. The Fool card gives you the courage to forge ahead.

Death

The Death card is not as ominous as it seems. Because it signifies transformation, it's an excellent card to wish on when you're really at a standstill and have nowhere to turn. Wishing on the Death card helps you to indicate to the universal energy that you're finished with all of your options and you would like this period to end and start again in a fresh new way. After meditating on the Death card, you may want to make your wishes on The Magician.

The Magician

This is the card of real transformation and new beginnings. If you're looking for a new approach to something or you want to understand how to handle a seemingly difficult situation, pick up The Magician, close your eyes, and imagine what it is you'd like to understand or attain. The Magician also means communication. If you wish to understand how you need to talk with someone or to get in touch with him or her, you can meditate with the Magician card and, it's hoped, come up with a clearer understanding of the situation.

The Wheel of Fortune

The Wheel of Fortune card is related to luck. If you don't know exactly which way you hope things will go (you only want them to turn out favorably), The Wheel of Fortune is the card you should wish on. Basically, you're asking for fate to be on your side. Sometimes, this is the only way to go—especially when you're not sure what you're actually hoping for.

Judgment

Since this card stands for fairness and correct judgment, you can wish for a positive outcome of any kind of legal affair. This works doubly well for a court hearing or trial. If your situation and your stance are valid, Judgment as a wish card will help tremendously.

Strength

This is the card of fortitude, strength, and courage. You can meditate and wish on this card for many things. It can help you make a decision that was previously not in your hands; it can also help you to gather the bravery you need for getting into a good situation or away from a bad one. The Strength card also has to do with sexual impulse. If you're attracted to someone, you can wish on the card; if you're attracted to someone and shouldn't be (or don't want to be), you can gather the force you need in order to move away from the source of the problem.

The Star

Of all the cards in the Major Arcana, this one is most appropriate for making a wish. Though it doesn't focus on any particular issue, this general wish card can be very potent. The good thing about The Star is that it makes things work out in your best interest, even if it's not in the way you intended it to happen.

The Star card as a wish tool sometimes works in strange ways. Though you don't necessarily come out with what you think you want, you definitely come out with the most positive results.

The World

Use The World to wish and meditate on for something of a higher spiritual purpose. It's a wonderful, beautiful symbol card that should be called upon not for controlling fate, but for accepting and encouraging it. In other words, if things are already going well, The World is a great card to meditate on in order to keep the good things going ahead.

The Emperor/The Empress

The Emperor/Empress cards are about taking your natural power in hand. The Emperor is an excellent wish card choice for a man who may want to tap into his masculine (or even nurturing) energy. The Empress card, on the other hand, can work well for a woman who wants to touch her female energy. As a wish card, this is the card that is extremely successful in regard to fertility and pregnancy. If you are hoping to conceive, The Empress is your wish card.

ALERT!

Runes and crystals are as powerful as the Tarot. Simply look up the meanings of each rune or crystal to use them as your tools for tapping into the positive wish energy.

Make It True

If you wish for something, can you make it happen? Why not? A positive attitude goes a long way toward getting what you want. And if you want something badly enough, it reflects in your actions and in your general outlook on life. Did you ever hear the phrase: "If you want something, you have to ask for it"? This should be applied to all areas of your life. Divination tells you what may happen. You're the one who's got to *make* it happen.

Meditation helps you put your desires out there, and you can use your divination tools, like the Tarot, runes, and crystals, to help you meditate. These powerful symbols can help you tap into universal energy, which you can influence.

Relying on Positive Energy

Because energy is affected by what you put into it, good psychics will tell you that when you're divining the future, it should come from a place of love and, of course, good intentions. Divination should never be about manipulating or controlling your fate. You should be gently touching and reading it.

Don't ever wish for bad things to happen to anyone. Remember karma—what goes around comes around. Let nature solve the problem. Karma works both ways. Whatever someone did to you will eventually come back to him or her.

Good psychics and mediums are spiritually evolved, stable, balanced, mentally healthy individuals. They have learned to forgive others, give generously (with love), and get rid of old baggage. The same goes for successful wishing—it must come from a positive stance.

Wishing on a Star

The future is actually more beautiful than you could have ever imagined it. How can this be true, with all of the problems, violence, and impossible situations we're faced with? We're tested in life each day. And yet there are some people who persevere and come out of every situation victorious. How do they do that? And how can we do the same? It's scary to try, and many of us put the task aside. After all, we're taught not to wish, and not to ask for something we want.

But what is it that these people do to get what they want so effortlessly? They have no great secret. In fact, a positive attitude probably brings them further than any trick you can think of.

You Can Make It Come True

"Wishing on a star" is a phrase synonymous with childhood and innocence. Chances are, when you were a child your parents told you that wishing on a star would help you get what you want. And so maybe you tried it, and when nothing happened, you soon gave up. But guess what? Wishing on a star is exactly what divination is. And it has to be done with good intentions in mind. It's not easy to be specific when dealing with something as awesome as universal energy. You can't just walk outside for two minutes, look up at the stars, and say, "I wish I could meet the woman of my dreams." You didn't take yourself or your wish seriously—why should the powers of the Earth?

Connecting with energy is like connecting with nature—it must be done carefully and methodically. Slowly. And by making the same wish every day, you come to an appreciation of the world and an awareness of your place in it. It's almost like meditating and protecting yourself before practicing divination. But it's even more sacred.

You should take at least an hour every evening to make your wish on a star. By focusing on the same star or group of stars, you can even ask for guidance or help with a problem you're having difficulty solving.

With wishing, there is nothing more important than understanding, honestly, what you really want (and not necessarily only what you need—go for the gold). Once you figure this out, you can sincerely ask for the best possible outcome of things. This is what "wishing on a star" is meant for. Does all of this sound "out there"? Are you skeptical, perhaps? Don't be.

Wishing on a star is one of the most influential forms of divination you can possibly perform. Admitting to your desires helps put thought into action for yourself; making your desires known gives the universal realm a way to actually materialize those dreams and desires for you. And there is nothing more powerful in divination than that.

Appendix A

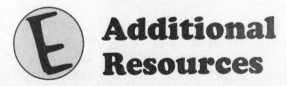

Additional Resources

Further Reading

Abadie, M.J. *The Everything® Angels Book*. Avon, MA: Adams Media Corporation, 2001.

Abadie, M.J. *The Everything® Tarot Book*. Avon, MA: Adams Media Corporation, 1999.

Abraham, Sylvia. *How to Use Tarot Spreads: Answers to Every Question*. St. Paul, MN: Llewellyn Worldwide, 1997.

Aswynn, Freya. *Principles of Runes*. London: Thorsons (HarperCollins Publishers), 2000.

Benitez, Armando. *Sheer Superstition: Outmaneuvering Fate*. Charlottesville, VA: Hampton Roads Publishing Company, 2000.

Bluestone, Sarvananda. *How to Read Signs and Omens in Everyday Life*. Rochester, VT: Destiny Books, 2002.

Burger, Everlyn and Johannes Fiebig. *Complete Book of Tarot Spreads*. New York: Sterling Publishing, 1997.

Burton, Sabrina. *The Lucky Book: Fun Predictions for Your Future*. Kansas City, MO: Andrews McMeel Publishing, 2001.

Conway, D.J. *Crystal Enchantments: A Complete Guide to Stones and Their Magical Properties*. Berkeley, CA: The Crossing Press, 2000.

Dening, Sarah. *The Everyday I Ching*. London: Simon & Schuster UK Ltd., 1995.

Diagram Group. *Predicting Your Future*. New York: Ballantine Books, 1994.

Donaldson, Terry. *Step by Step Tarot: A Complete Guide in Tarot Readership*. Thorsons (HarperCollins Publishers), 1994.

Ducie, Sonia. *Sonia Ducie's Numerology Secrets*. London: Thorsons (HarperCollins Publishers), 2000.

Eason, Cassandra. *Complete Guide to Divination: How to Use the Most Popular Methods of Fortune Telling*. London: Piatkus Books, 1998.

González-Wippler, Migene. *Dreams and What They Mean to You*. St. Paul, MN: Llewellyn Publications, 2001.

Hall, Judy. *The Illustrated Guide to Divination: A Practical Guide to Predicting the Future.* New York: Sterling Publishing, 2000.

Harris, Eleanor L. *Ancient Egyptian Divination and Magic.* York Beach, ME: Red Wheel/Weiser, 1998.

Hewitt, William W. *Tea Leaf Reading.* St. Paul, MN: Llewellyn Publications, 1989.

King, Francis X. *Encyclopedia of Fortune Telling.* London: Hamlyn, 1999.

Knight, Sirona. *The Little Giant Encyclopedia of Runes.* New York: Sterling Publishing, 2000.

Lily, Simon. *Crystal Healing.* London: Anness Publishing Ltd., 1999.

Linn, Denise. *The Secret Language of Signs.* New York: Ballantine Books (Random House), 1996.

Little Gift Books. *The Mystery of Runes.* Kansas City, MO: Andrews McMeel Publishing, 1998.

Lyle, Jane. *The Cup of Destiny.* London: Connections Book Publishing Ltd., 2000.

MacGregor, Trish. *The Everything® Astrology Book.* Avon, MA: Adams Media Corporation, 1998.

MacGregor, Trish and Rob MacGregor. *The Everything® Dreams Book.* Avon, MA: Adams Media Corporation, 1997.

Margolis, Char. *Questions from Earth, Answers from Heaven.* New York: St. Martin's Press, 1999.

Morningstar, Sally. *Divining the Future.* New York: Lorenz Books (Anness Publishing, Ltd.), 2000.

Morag, Hali. *Playing Cards: Predicting Your Future.* Hod Hasharon, Israel: Astrolog Publishing House, 1998.

Naylor, Peter. *Discovering Dowsing and Divining.* Risborough, Buckinghamshire, England: Shire Publications Ltd., 1997.

Nostradamus and Ned Halley, ed. *The Complete Prophecies of Nostradamus.* Hertfordshire, England: Wordsworth Editions Ltd., 1999.

Peschel, Lisa. *A Practical Guide to the Runes*. St. Paul, MN: Llewellyn Publications, 1989.

Reed, Ellen Cannon. *The Heart of Wicca: Wise Words from a Crone on the Path*. York Beach, ME: Red Wheel/Weiser, 2000.

Sofia (Mystic). *Fortune Telling with Playing Cards*. St. Paul, MN: Llewellyn Publications, 1996.

Sorrell, Roderic and Amy Max Sorrell. *The I Ching Made Easy*. San Francisco, CA: HarperSanFrancisco, 1994.

Smythe, J. *The Complete Book of Fortune-telling*. New York: Gramercy Books, 1998.

Struthers, Jane. *Read Your Future: The Ultimate Guide to Tarot, Astrology, the I Ching, and Other Divination Techniques from Around the World*. New York: St. Martin's Press, 2002.

Thorsson, Edred. *The Runecaster's Handbook: The Well of Wyrd*. York Beach, ME: Red Wheel/Weiser, 1999.

Too, Lillian. *Lillian Too's Smart Feng Shui for the Home*. Thorsons (HarperCollins Publishers), 2001.

Tyson, Donald. *Scrying for Beginners: Tapping into the Supersensory Powers of Your Subconscious*. St. Paul, MN: Llewellyn Publications, 1997.

Upczak, Patricia Rose. *Synchronicity, Signs & Symbols*. Nederland, CO: Synchronicity Publishing, 2001.

Waite, A.E. *The Key to the Tarot*. London: Random House U.K. Ltd., 1999 (first published in 1910).

Webster, Richard. *The Complete Book of Palmistry: Includes Secrets of Indian Thumb Reading*. St. Paul, MN: Llewellyn, 2001.

Wilhelm, Richard. *The Pocket I Ching, the Richard Wilhelm Translation*. London: Routledge & Kegan Paul Ltd., 1984.

Wilhelm, Richard (editor); C. G. Jung (foreword); Cary F. Baynes (translator). *The I Ching: Or Book of Changes*. New York: Arkana, 1989.

Zehavi, Sarah. *All About Predicting the Future*. Hod Hasharon, Israel: Astrolog Publishing House, 2000.

Psychic Web Sites

Candle Therapy

This Web site, maintained by Dr. Catherine Riggs-Bergesen, a licensed clinical psychologist, offers many interesting articles on magic and divination. Dr. Riggs-Bergesen is also the owner of Other Worldly Waxes, a candle therapy shop based in downtown New York City. Products available include Tarot decks, oils, incenses, books on divination, and so forth. If you want real magic, click on the "magic candle" box and order a personally designed, hand-carved Wicca candle (made by in-house professionals or Catherine herself) that you can burn in the privacy of your home. They're great for helping a sick friend or family member, for career or money decisions and problems, and for love and relationship issues. Visit the Candle Therapy site at ✍ *www.candletherapy.com.*

E-mail Psychics.com

E-mail readings offered here are inexpensive, about $10, and fast—you should get a response within twenty-four hours. These e-mails won't be as detailed and personal as readings from the other recommended sites, but payment is secure and it's convenient. If you'd like a quick reading, log on at ✍ *www.emailpsychic.com.*

Global Psychics

This Web site features a group of women, who are psychics and therapists. Their methods are wonderful and you'll receive pages of information, which you can then save and read again at a later date. Analyses are in-depth and helpful; credit card payments are made on a secure page. They offer advice from career and money to lifestyle, higher "self" analysis, and even readings for you and your pet. "Group readings," each done separately by different psychics, is a good way to go; you'll get three times the information and three points of view. Visit the Global Psychics at ✍ *www.globalpsychics.com.*

Love Psychics

This Web site is similar to Global Psychics, but it's operated in Canada. This site is highly recommended for its e-mail readings as well as on-the-spot chat readings. Payment is secure. Visit the Love Psychics at ✍ *www.lovepsychics.com.*

Psychics & Mediums Network

This clever Web site is brought to you from England by a well-known, well-respected psychic and author. These psychics use methods such as crystals, runes, or the Tarot. Visit the Psychics & Mediums Network at ✍ *www.psychics.co.uk.*

E-mail for a Personal Reading

Lynn Miller

Outgoing, funny, and talented, Lynn has clients from all over, including celebrities (she's based in Los Angeles, California). Lynn is psychic and does not rely on divination props of any kind. Book in advance—she's always busy—at *Millerangl1469@aol.com.*

Randy Jones

Randy's been extremely booked lately but if you get a hold of him, he's the Tarot master, and a great guy. He also does in-depth readings over the phone. You can ask any and all questions—e-mail him at *RaThJo3471@aol.com.*

Jenni Kosarin

I am based in Florence, Italy, but I help clients from all over, through e-mail and phone readings. My specialty is the Tarot, and I give fantastic advice—especially on career and love. You can also e-mail me if you have questions or comments about this book. Get in touch with me at *Jkosarin@aol.com.*

Appendix B

Glossary

A

AIR SIGNS:

Gemini, Libra, or Aquarius.

ANGEL:

A spiritual being of light who guides you in life.

ARITHOMANCY:

Divination performed through the use of numbers; also called NUMEROLOGY and numeromancy.

ASTROLOGY:

A method of divining the future from the position of the stars, the moon, and the sun according to your birth date.

AUGURY:

Though it normally refers to divination through the patterns made by birds, it also means divination practiced by watching the behavior of animals.

AURA:

The glow of light surrounding a person that projects (and affects) his image. For the majority of psychics, the aura of a person is hard to detect. Each person has a different colored aura.

AUTOMATIC WRITING:

Divination done through the use of spirits. The writing comes through the spiritual entity's imagination/memory, not your own.

B

BIRTH CHART:

Also known as the natal chart or HOROSCOPE, it helps determine personality characteristics based on the placement of the sun, the moon, and the planets at the time of birth.

C

CHAKRA:

Region of energy in the body; when it malfunctions, you may cleanse it with crystal energy.

CHANNELER:

A medium; someone who connects with spirit entities through her aura.

CHIROMANCY:

Palmistry or palm reading—performing divination and character/personality analyses by reading finger and hand shapes as well as palm lines and markings.

CLAIRAUDIENCE:

Hearing sounds from the future.

CLAIRVOYANCE:

Seeing things before they happen; visions of the future.

CRYSTALLOMANCY:

Using a crystal ball in order to see into the future.

CRYSTALS:

Powerful gemstones of the earth used for divination, healing, and meditation.

CUPS:

A suit of the Tarot that refers to happiness or emotional matters and the water sun signs. In terms of time, Cups can also refer to days.

D

DOWSING:

A method of divination used for finding lost articles through magnetic vibrations; locating anything under the earth.

E

EARTH SIGNS:
Capricorn, Taurus, or Virgo.

THE ELDER FUTHARK:
An Ancient German alphabet used for the symbols of the runes that begins with the letters F, U, Th, A, R, and K.

ELEMENTS:
Fire, air, water, and earth.

ESP (EXTRA SENSORY PERCEPTION):
Knowing or having a strong feeling something is going to happen; sixth sense.

F

FIRE SIGNS:
Leo, Aries, or Sagittarius.

FREE WILL:
The choice that everyone has to change one's destiny.

G

GEOMANCY:
Divination with substances of the earth (like soil and sand).

GRAPHOLOGY:
Divination practiced through analyzing a person's handwriting.

H

HEXAGRAM:
A chart composed of six lines; it refers to the six throws of three coins in order to divine the future using the I CHING. Hexagrams are constructed from the bottom up.

HOROSCOPE:
Zodiac or birth/natal chart.

HYDROMANCY:
Divination or SCRYING with water.

I

I CHING:
The Book of Changes, an ancient Chinese oracle method of divination done by throwing three coins and constructing HEXAGRAMS.

K

KARMA:
Best described by the phrase "what goes around comes around"—if you do something good, it will come back to you. The Buddhists believe that your karma is carried over from lifetime to lifetime.

L

LIFE LESSONS:
What you need to learn in order for your soul to evolve and move forward.

LITHOMANCY:
Divination with CRYSTALS—gemstones of the earth.

M

MAJOR ARCANA:
The twenty-two picture cards in the Tarot (such as The Fool, The Devil, Judgment, and so on) that are fate/destiny cards. They refer to things that are bound to happen.

MINOR ARCANA:
Cards in the Tarot deck that are divided into four suits: CUPS, PENTACLES, SWORDS, and WANDS.

N

NECROMANCY:

Divination through the dead (spirits), which may include using the Ouija board, conducting a séance, and automatic writing.

NUMEROLOGY:

Also called numeromancy and ARITHOMANCY—divination and character analysis done through the use of numbers.

O

OENOMANCY:

Divination performed by reading the lees (dregs) of wine.

ONEIROMANCY:

A method of divining the future done by analyzing dreams.

ORACLE:

An advice form of divination, such as the I Ching and runes.

OUIJA BOARD:

A board with the letters of the alphabet, numbers, and Yes, No, and Goodbye, used to contact spiritual entities. Messages are spelled out letter by letter.

P

PALMISTRY:

See CHIROMANCY.

PENTACLES:

In the Tarot, Pentacles refer to the earth sun signs and signify money, stability, and security. In terms of time, Pentacles represent years.

PHRENOLOGY:

Divination performed by examining the bumps and indentations on a person's head.

PLANCHETTE:

The device employed by those using the Ouija board; it skims across the surface and points to the letters and numbers indicated by the spirits.

PRECOGNITION:

Knowing something is going to happen in the future; sensing something beforehand.

PSYCHOMETRY:

Divining past, present, or future events by touching an object or someone's possession.

PYROMANCY:

Divination through the use of fire.

Q

QUERENT:

The person who asks the question in a reading.

R

READING:

Looking into the future by casting, throwing, or SCRYING.

RUNES:

Ancient letters now used in divination. Each symbol is painted on natural materials such as stone or wood.

S

SCRYING:

Seeing into the future by use of a shiny, unmoving surface, like a crystal ball or a pool of water.

SÉANCE:

A form of divination used for connecting with spiritual entities.

SPIRIT GUIDE:
Teacher, angel, or helper in spiritual form.

SPIRITUAL WORLD:
All of the other planes and dimensions besides our known universe.

SPREAD:
A layout of the runes, Tarot, or crystals made in order to divine the future.

SUN SIGN:
Birth sign—the house of the zodiac (there are twelve houses) where the sun was located at the time of your birth.

SWORDS:
In the Tarot, Swords are connected to air signs and refer to mental processes and suffering. In terms of time, Swords represent months.

T

TAROT:
A deck of cards in which each symbolizes one part of the universal stages of life. There are many different packs of Tarot cards; they are used for meditation and divination.

TASSEOGRAPHY:
Divination performed by reading the symbols found in leftover tealeaves in a teacup.

TASSEOMANCY:
See TASSEOGRAPHY.

W

WANDS:
In the Tarot, Wands refer to fire signs and signify spiritual development and moving forward. In terms of time, Wands represent weeks.

WATER SIGNS:
Cancer, Scorpio, and Pisces.

Index

THE EVERYTHING® ASTROLOGY BOOK

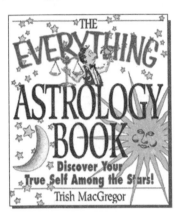

By Trish MacGregor

The Everything® Astrology Book is a primer to the mysterious, often surprising world of astrology. While most of use know what sign we were born under, we only see its relation to ourselves in the context of the pithy comments found in newspapers or magazines. But these brief remarks don't tell the whole story. In this book, you'll quickly discover what your sign means, how to use your sign's inherent characteristics to your advantage, which signs are most compatible, how to choose a career that best suits you, and more!

Trade paperback,
$14.95 ($22.95 CAN)
1-58062-062-0, 320 pages

OTHER *EVERYTHING®* BOOKS BY ADAMS MEDIA CORPORATION

BUSINESS

Everything® **Business Planning Book**
Everything® **Coaching & Mentoring Book**
Everything® **Home-Based Business Book**
Everything® **Leadership Book**
Everything® **Managing People Book**
Everything® **Network Marketing Book**
Everything® **Online Business Book**
Everything® **Project Management Book**
Everything® **Selling Book**
Everything® **Start Your Own Business Book**
Everything® **Time Management Book**

COMPUTERS

Everything® **Build Your Own Home Page Book**
Everything® **Computer Book**

Everything® **Internet Book**
Everything® **Microsoft® Word 2000 Book**

COOKING

Everything® **Barbecue Cookbook**
Everything® **Bartender's Book, $9.95**
Everything® **Chocolate Cookbook**
Everything® **Cookbook**
Everything® **Dessert Cookbook**
Everything® **Diabetes Cookbook**
Everything® **Low-Carb Cookbook**
Everything® **Low-Fat High-Flavor Cookbook**
Everything® **Mediterranean Cookbook**
Everything® **One-Pot Cookbook**
Everything® **Pasta Book**
Everything® **Quick Meals Cookbook**
Everything® **Slow Cooker Cookbook**

Everything® **Soup Cookbook**
Everything® **Thai Cookbook**
Everything® **Vegetarian Cookbook**
Everything® **Wine Book**

HEALTH

Everything® **Anti-Aging Book**
Everything® **Dieting Book**
Everything® **Herbal Remedies Book**
Everything® **Hypnosis Book**
Everything® **Menopause Book**
Everything® **Nutrition Book**
Everything® **Stress Management Book**
Everything®**Vitamins, Minerals, and Nutritional Supplements Book**

HISTORY

Everything® **American History Book**

All Everything® books are priced at $12.95 or $14.95, unless otherwise stated. Prices subject to change without notice.
Canadian prices range from $11.95–$22.95 and are subject to change without notice.

Everything® **Civil War Book**
Everything® **World War II Book**

HOBBIES

Everything® **Bridge Book**
Everything® **Candlemaking Book**
Everything® **Casino Gambling Book**
Everything® **Chess Basics Book**
Everything® **Collectibles Book**
Everything® **Crossword and Puzzle Book**
Everything® **Digital Photography Book**
Everything® **Drums Book (with CD),**
    $19.95, ($31.95 CAN)
Everything® **Family Tree Book**
Everything® **Games Book**
Everything® **Guitar Book**
Everything® **Knitting Book**
Everything® **Magic Book**
Everything® **Motorcycle Book**
Everything® **Online Genealogy Book**
Everything® **Playing Piano and**
    Keyboards Book
Everything® **Rock & Blues Guitar**
    Book (with CD), $19.95,
    ($31.95 CAN)
Everything® **Scrapbooking Book**

HOME IMPROVEMENT

Everything® **Feng Shui Book**
Everything® **Gardening Book**
Everything® **Home Decorating Book**
Everything® **Landscaping Book**
Everything® **Lawn Care Book**
Everything® **Organize Your Home Book**

KIDS' STORY BOOKS

Everything® **Bedtime Story Book**
Everything® **Bible Stories Book**
Everything® **Fairy Tales Book**
Everything® **Mother Goose Book**

NEW AGE

Everything® **Astrology Book**

Everything® **Divining the Future Book**
Everything® **Dreams Book**
Everything® **Ghost Book**
Everything® **Meditation Book**
Everything® **Numerology Book**
Everything® **Palmistry Book**
Everything® **Spells and Charms Book**
Everything® **Tarot Book**
Everything® **Wicca and Witchcraft Book**

PARENTING

Everything® **Baby Names Book**
Everything® **Baby Shower Book**
Everything® **Baby's First Food Book**
Everything® **Baby's First Year Book**
Everything® **Breastfeeding Book**
Everything® **Get Ready for Baby Book**
Everything® **Homeschooling Book**
Everything® **Potty Training Book,**
    $9.95, ($15.95 CAN)
Everything® **Pregnancy Book**
Everything® **Pregnancy Organizer,**
    $15.00, ($22.95 CAN)
Everything® **Toddler Book**
Everything® **Tween Book**

PERSONAL FINANCE

Everything® **Budgeting Book**
Everything® **Get Out of Debt Book**
Everything® **Get Rich Book**
Everything® **Investing Book**
Everything® **Homebuying Book, 2nd Ed.**
Everything® **Homeselling Book**
Everything® **Money Book**
Everything® **Mutual Funds Book**
Everything® **Online Investing Book**
Everything® **Personal Finance Book**

PETS

Everything® **Cat Book**
Everything® **Dog Book**
Everything® **Dog Training and Tricks**
Everything® **Horse Book**
Everything® **Puppy Book**
Everything® **Tropical Fish Book**

REFERENCE

Everything® **Astronomy Book**
Everything® **Car Care Book**
Everything® **Christmas Book, $15.00,**
    ($21.95 CAN)
Everything® **Classical Mythology Book**
Everything® **Divorce Book**
Everything® **Etiquette Book**
Everything® **Great Thinkers Book**
Everything® **Learning French Book**
Everything® **Learning German Book**
Everything® **Learning Italian Book**
Everything® **Learning Latin Book**
Everything® **Learning Spanish Book**
Everything® **Mafia Book**
Everything® **Philosophy Book**
Everything® **Shakespeare Book**
Everything® **Tall Tales, Legends, &**
    Other Outrageous Lies Book
Everything® **Toasts Book**
Everything® **Trivia Book**
Everything® **Weather Book**
Everything® **Wills & Estate Planning**
    Book

RELIGION

Everything® **Angels Book**
Everything® **Buddhism Book**
Everything® **Catholicism Book**
Everything® **Judaism Book**
Everything® **Saints Book**
Everything® **World's Religions Book**
Everything® **Understanding Islam Book**

SCHOOL & CAREERS

Everything® **After College Book**
Everything® **College Survival Book**
Everything® **Cover Letter Book**
Everything® **Get-a-Job Book**
Everything® **Hot Careers Book**
Everything® **Job Interview Book**
Everything® **Online Job Search Book**
Everything® **Resume Book, 2nd Ed.**
Everything® **Study Book**

All Everything® books are priced at $12.95 or $14.95, unless otherwise stated. Prices subject to change without notice.
Canadian prices range from $11.95–$22.95 and are subject to change without notice.

WE HAVE EVERYTHING . . . .

SPORTS/FITNESS

Everything® **Bicycle Book**
Everything® **Fishing Book**
Everything® **Fly-Fishing Book**
Everything® **Golf Book**
Everything® **Golf Instruction Book**
Everything® **Pilates Book**
Everything® **Running Book**
Everything® **Sailing Book, 2nd Ed.**
Everything® **T'ai Chi and QiGong Book**
Everything® **Total Fitness Book**
Everything® **Weight Training Book**
Everything® **Yoga Book**

TRAVEL

Everything® **Guide to Las Vegas**
Everything® **Guide to New England**
Everything® **Guide to New York City**
Everything® **Guide to Washington D.C.**

Everything® **Travel Guide to The Disneyland Resort®, California Adventure®, Universal Studios®, and the Anaheim Area**
Everything® **Travel Guide to the Walt Disney World® Resort, Universal Studios®, and Greater Orlando, 3rd Ed.**

WEDDINGS & ROMANCE

Everything® **Creative Wedding Ideas Book**
Everything® **Dating Book**
Everything® **Jewish Wedding Book**
Everything® **Romance Book**
Everything® **Wedding Book, 2nd Ed.**
Everything® **Wedding Organizer, $15.00** ($22.95 CAN)

Everything® **Wedding Checklist,** $7.95 ($11.95 CAN)
Everything® **Wedding Etiquette Book,** $7.95 ($11.95 CAN)
Everything® **Wedding Shower Book,** $7.95 ($12.95 CAN)
Everything® **Wedding Vows Book,** $7.95 ($11.95 CAN)
Everything® **Weddings on a Budget Book, $9.95** ($15.95 CAN)

WRITING

Everything® **Creative Writing Book**
Everything® **Get Published Book**
Everything® **Grammar and Style Book**
Everything® **Grant Writing Book**
Everything® **Guide to Writing Children's Books**
Everything® **Writing Well Book**

ALSO AVAILABLE:
THE EVERYTHING® KIDS' SERIES!

Each book is 8" x 9¼", 144 pages, and two-color throughout.

Everything® **Kids' Baseball Book, 2nd Edition, $6.95** ($10.95 CAN)
Everything® **Kids' Bugs Book, $6.95** ($10.95 CAN)
Everything® **Kids' Cookbook, $6.95** ($10.95 CAN)
Everything® **Kids' Joke Book, $6.95** ($10.95 CAN)
Everything® **Kids' Math Puzzles Book, $6.95** ($10.95 CAN)
Everything® **Kids' Mazes Book, $6.95** ($10.95 CAN)
Everything® **Kids' Money Book, $6.95** ($11.95 CAN)

Everything® **Kids' Monsters Book, $6.95** ($10.95 CAN)
Everything® **Kids' Nature Book, $6.95** ($11.95 CAN)
Everything® **Kids' Puzzle Book $6.95,** ($10.95 CAN)
Everything® **Kids' Science Experiments Book, $6.95** ($10.95 CAN)
Everything® **Kids' Soccer Book, $6.95** ($10.95 CAN)
Everything® **Kids' Travel Activity Book, $6.95** ($10.95 CAN)